Rushion,
Life is a...
Living is a Choice...
Live to the fullest en
all you do!
Blessings,
Nicole

Matter

A WOMAN'S
True
PURPOSE

DR. NICOLE LaBEACH

SOURCEBOOKS, INC.®
NAPERVILLE, ILLINOIS

Published by Sourcebooks, Inc.
P.O. Box 4410, Naperville, Illinois 60567-4410
(630) 961-3900
FAX: (630) 961-2168
www.sourcebooks.com

Library of Congress Cataloging-in-Publication Data
LaBeach, Nicole.
  A Woman's True Purpose: Live Like You Matter / Nicole LaBeach.
     p. cm.
  ISBN-13: 978-1-4022-0730-3
  ISBN-10: 1-4022-0730-1
  1.   Christian women—Religious life. 2.   Self-Realization—Religious
aspects—Christianity. I. Title.

BV4527.L23 2007
248.8'43—dc22

                                                      2006100908

Printed and bound in the United States of America
        VP 10 9 8 7 6 5 4 3 2 1

Dedication

I gladly dedicate this work to my Lord and Savior Jesus Christ. How grateful I am to know and be in a relationship with you. May the words of my mouth and the meditations of my heart be forever acceptable in thy sight. To my husband and my mother, you make the difference. I love and thank you both for everything.

Table of Contents

Introduction

How different would life be if you treated yourself as your best asset? If you recognized how valuable you are as a woman? If you embraced purpose, fulfillment, and wholeness as necessities for living?

Why is the routine of waking up and wanting more for our lives so predictable?

Life is a gift. So why aren't we living as if it were the best gift we've ever received? Why is the routine of waking up and wanting more for our lives so predictable? If life is a gift, what is living? We have remedies and fix-its for everything under the sun, yet living like we matter seems elusive. The type of living that celebrates a strong spiritual relationship, purpose-driven choices, and personal fulfillment is not what we often choose.

Throughout time, society has encouraged men to engage in activities that promote personal evolvement, fulfillment, and self-preservation. Women, on the other hand, are often required to fight for their right to choose and frequently learn to engage in behaviors that are more self-destructive than self-actualizing. In a time when women are still fighting for the right to equality, democracy, and self governance, it is important that we start to choose to live passionately in all of the fullness God will afford.

Though many of us have defined our womanhood by the ability to place our personal needs, aspirations, and potential behind that of others, we must begin to put an end to the continuous denial of our own purpose, passion, and brilliance. We must choose to embrace the greatness of our God-given worth and see how choosing to live like we matter is one of our most critical assignments. Wholeness is the key to giving love to others in an abundant and authentic manner; however, this choice seems to be the one we struggle with the most. Though we can't give what we don't have, many of us have become pros at being everything to others while giving little or nothing to ourselves. As a result, the diligence with which many of us care for ourselves is often minimal. It's simple but yet so complex: As women, we must begin to acknowledge, own, and embrace the right to live like we matter.

LIVING LIKE YOU MATTER REQUIRES YOU
TO BE LOVING TOWARD YOURSELF AND
EXPECT PERSONAL GREATNESS FROM
YOURSELF AS A PREREQUISITE FOR GIVING
YOUR BEST TO ANYONE ELSE.

In our attempts to be selfless we've forgotten that personal purpose, growth, and fulfillment are great gifts we can proudly extend to our loved ones and the rest of humanity. Unfortunately, many of us have no real concept of what real living is. This is a major issue. The problem for most of us is not the results gained from living, but the process required to get to it. Living like you matter requires you to be loving toward yourself and expect personal greatness from yourself as a prerequisite for giving your best to anyone else. This is the part that's usually too much for us to handle. This is by no means an "all about self" philosophy, it's a "woman, love, regard, and heal thyself emergency"!

As women, we've all experienced threats to our sense of self and self-worth. The intense stress, suppressed anger, secret insecurities, deep-rooted fears, and unresolved issues that plague our everyday lives often make wholeness and internal happiness seem impossible to achieve. As we try to seek shortcuts (e.g., material things outside of ourselves) to contentment, many of us have recognized there are none. Why? Because true internal happiness is not derived from things outside of ourselves—instead it manifests from an ability to feel good from the inside out. Of course we all experience moments of joy, but true contentment stems from a strong sense of spiritual and inner peace. It manifests from an authentic love and acceptance of self. It comes from a strong spiritual connection which affords us the ability to embrace who we are, whose we are, what we want, and what we mean to the world.

Though it may seem daunting, fulfillment is probably the one thing we have the most control over because it starts with us. It comes from an acceptance of who you are as a child of God, an acknowledgment that you possess a unique significance, and the power to choose change and forgiveness. With one life, one spirit, one mind, and one body, we cannot afford to continue doubting this truth.

WE MAY SMILE A LOT AND ACQUIRE OUR SHARE OF STATUS SYMBOLS, BUT NOTHING WILL CHANGE THE FEELING THAT WE'RE NOT FULLY LIVING EXCEPT THE DECISION TO START LIVING LIKE WE MATTER.

As women, we must embrace that a fundamental aspect of our inability to achieve personal fulfillment stems from our inability to choose ourselves (emotional, spiritual, relational, and physical health). We may smile a lot and acquire our share of status symbols, but nothing will change the feeling that we're not fully living except the decision to start living like we matter. For many of us, the desire to live a fulfilled life is a consistent one, however, this is met with great difficulty because most of us have yet to master the ability to choose ourselves (e.g., stop beating up on ourselves, stop putting everyone else's needs before our own, and start living a life that embraces personal purpose). In its essence, it's an exercise in caring for your best and most important asset—you.

A Woman's True Purpose offers Seven Steps to Living Like You Matter. This seven-step approach will encourage and solidify insight to help you identify, understand, and move within an authentic depiction of your unique personal power and possibilities as a woman. As a journey, it promises to promote clarity, understanding, and the removal of obstructions that serve to halt your personal progress.

With authority, Step One: Believe the Power of Your God-View, sheds light on the discrepancy between who you think you are and who God says you are. Through affording a tangible approach to looking at yourself, Step One is a wake-up call—one that starts where you are and offers liberation through going back to the simple beginning where the truth resides. It offers the recognition that there is an original and empowered definition of who you are that doesn't define your worth by anything other than how you were initially created. It affords a definition that is free of personal self-doubt and unhealthy critical influence. As a strong foundation, it sets the stage for your journey to the next step.

Step Two: Take Charge of Your Past, is a take-no-prisoners approach to revisiting the past and coming through with a bona fide sense of your "her-story." Through learning to travel light and take dominion over your past, Step Two introduces the power of taking authority over people, places, things, and negative moments of impact that serve to obstruct your path. It will ask that you make the sometimes painful observation of dead weight that needs to be removed. It will also give you a critical opportunity to move beyond the deceptive belief that moments of impact have the power to define you. This confrontation with the past will give you the forethought needed to progress forward.

Having moved to Step Three: Embrace the Potential of Resolution, you will have an opportunity to look at two of the master teachers in your life (your mother/mother figure and father/father figure) and see how their choices and lack of resolution in relationships affect movement in your own personal journey. These chapters will help you see how the idea of choosing yourself may have been derailed at an early age. With a greater understanding of these dynamics, you'll be better equipped to achieve resolution in your present relationships that need it.

When you complete Step Three you will be well prepared to take Step Four: Stop Being Invisible. Offering a navigation system for love and how to remove unrealistic self demands, Step Four will help you take control of elements that seek to compound your life. Through a close look at superwomanhood—the state of being and doing all things to and for all people, this step presents an opportunity to check yourself into superwoman recovery and explore the process in all that it entails. It not only addresses the connection between wholeness and getting the mate you want but it also looks at maintaining that sense of balance once you've found that special someone.

Having completed Steps One through Four, Step Five: Move in the Divine Direction invites you to move in the optimal direction. In honoring the unique desire in your heart, this step asks the question "What does your heart say?" and it dares you to celebrate the answer. It challenges you to see your personal purpose through what is considered the Live Like You Matter "Heart" approach. It also serves to help you understand what can or may have thrown you off the divine path. Positioning you to declare your vision, it will reveal how your attitude and expectations will serve to influence its manifestation.

With a more substantial view of the woman you were born to be, Step Six: Get in the Moment, It's All You've Got, asks that you allow yourself to consciously engage in the critical moments of your life. Through confronting adversity, this step will place you in a face-to-face conversation with your fears and promote the option of moving regardless of their presence. You'll see how rushing through your life serves to distract you from the things God wants you to pay attention to and how it ultimately affects reaching your purpose driven destination. Through thought provoking ideas, this step will show you how denouncing your personal power equates to standing on the sidelines of your own life.

Once you've moved through Step Six, your preparedness for Step Seven: Renew Your Sweet Spot, will feel like a natural progression. This last and final step promises to bring you full circle and renew your "Sweet Spot"—the place from which all blessings flow for those who are willing to show up to get it.

As you go through the steps of this book, the journey toward the real you, the fulfilled you, will be easier to travel. As a vehicle of self-discovery, be ready to take ownership of where you are and declare where you want to go. As you read, take the time to digest the Seven Critical Reminders and complete the Insight Corner at the end of every chapter. These critical and insightful questions were created to customize your journey. Though you can read through and choose not to write a word, seeing your thoughts articulated on paper is a powerful tool of healing and revelation that should never be underestimated. Doing so promises to change your entire reading experience. So without further ado, dare to discover your true purpose and start living like you matter!

BELIEVE THE POWER OF YOUR GOD-VIEW

Chapter 1:

YOUR SELF-VIEW HAS MUCH TO DO WITH EVERYTHING

"HOW COULD THIS BE HAPPENING? I've tried everything, yet I feel like I'm on a treadmill going nowhere."

At one point in my life, I thought joy and the moon were an equal distance away from where I was standing. What else was there? I had racked up one accomplishment after another yet…what was I missing? These were questions I couldn't get away from. And why couldn't I use my trusty tools of overcompensation, overachievement, and plain old denial to pretend I found what I wanted? Why was happiness so hard to attain? Seriously, what was I missing?

Then my inner voice made a suggestion—yourself. "That's impossible, I protested. I'm with her every day." As if my inner voice were the enemy, I just refused to believe it. This voice tried to say the same thing for years, but I never chose to listen. Unfortunately, the biggest adversary for my spiritual inner voice was me.

Year in and year out, I had every excuse in the book on why I was unhappy: If I had…If I knew then…If I could…The fact of the matter was, I didn't think enough of myself and what God had created in me to move my life in any other direction than the mediocre one I settled for. Back then it was easier to place my power in the hands of everything else to explain why I felt unfulfilled. Time and time again, I attempted to fix the surface—new clothes, new look, new job, new network—yet wondered why my efforts always failed to reach my heart. At the time I didn't realize the problem was my unhappiness with myself.

Though I could have prayed for guidance, I felt like broaching the subject of unhappiness would be an act of complaining or being unappreciative for all God had done in my life. I prayed about everything else except happiness. And, on the rare occasion I listened to my heart, I was eager to discourage any feelings it might reveal. Like a dog chasing its tail, I went around and around in circles convinced I needed to do something different, but I was never quite sure what.

Then, I just got tired. I got tired of faking happiness, searching for fulfillment, crying through my feeling of emptiness, and missing the mark. Most of all, I was sick and tired of the subtle reminders that made it clear I wasn't fully experiencing my own life. Every time I achieved a goal I found little joy in it. Every time I was told I had "a blessed life," I just couldn't see it as such. Every time I failed to see in myself what others, not to mention God, saw in me, I was reminded that something wasn't quite right. Having tried everything else, I figured why not start with the end in mind by assessing where I was in relation to where I wanted to go in life. What did I have to lose? I now know that the question should have been: What did I need to lose?

I LOOKED AT MYSELF EVERY DAY
IN THE MIRROR BUT IT NEVER OCCURRED
TO ME TO THANK HER, SMILE AT HER,
ADMIRE HER, COMPLIMENT HER,
ENCOURAGE HER, AND CHERISH HER
FOR ALL THAT SHE HAD BEEN
AS MY GOD-GIVEN REFLECTION.

Looking back, I can say with authority that I forgive myself for all the time I spent searching in all the wrong places. It never occurred to me that I already had what I needed to achieve a true sense of happiness. Like so many women, I continuously looked outside of myself to find what was located within.

Truthfully, the weak part of me thought my life at that time was just the way it was going to be. We often resign ourselves to the thought of accepting the status quo. But the stronger part told me this wasn't all there was. So I challenged myself to accept that maybe, just maybe, I had more inside than I ever gave myself credit for. I accumulated so much emotional baggage, I couldn't see my way clear to what I had. I looked at myself every day in the mirror but it never occurred to me to thank her, smile at her, admire her, compliment her, encourage her, and cherish her for all that she had been as my God-given reflection. Didn't she deserve that? You would think so, since, like you, my reflection had been with me long before my first bra, boyfriend, or job. Instead, not seeing who I was was just another part of the routine. I was moving too fast to take a good look at myself, my life, or God's love for me. Why was that so difficult?

NO ONE WAS WILLING TO DECLARE THAT CHEATING OURSELVES OF SELF-LOVE LED TO CHEATING EVERYONE AROUND US.

Like many of us, I had a fundamental problem. I wasn't being the best to myself because I didn't think the best of myself and I couldn't see who I was, whose I was, or who I was born to be. Up until then, I had heard a great deal about self-esteem, but I really didn't get it. I didn't make the connection—how I felt about myself was a factor in how I was experiencing my life. Too often, I was overly critical, unforgiving, and unreasonable to myself.

Part of the reason it didn't occur to me was the fact that most women didn't seem to love themselves. On any given day, I could find more women beating up on themselves than not. We all knew we were struggling with the same thing, but no one truthfully talked about it. No one was willing to declare that cheating ourselves of self-love led to cheating everyone around us. What I realized was that I was a proud member of an unspoken club of millions of women. I was not alone. There was always another woman putting herself last on the list or stretching herself way too thin. This one would battle feelings of unworthiness, while that one prided herself on being a people-pleaser, secretly believing she was just faking being good enough. And that was the short list.

Daughters, wives, girlfriends, mothers, and sisters were all members of a club that taught others how to treat us by how we treated ourselves. If we always pushed the envelope, never said no, suppressed our personal needs and dreams, and tried to be all things to all people, then we were following the club's bylaws. How could that be? How could these choices be such a common thread connecting me to so many other women? And how did we justify using these yardsticks to measure the worth of each other though it was tearing each of us down on the inside?

I realized then, I had adopted disregard for myself as one of the secret access passes to womanhood. Despite being an independent, educated, and ambitious woman, I didn't see valuing my spiritual, emotional, physical, and relational health as a priority. The goodness inside myself was the key. I couldn't give my best without celebrating the value of my own human spirit.

For each of us, true living requires that we embrace life as one that is filled with endless possibilities. However, it is very difficult to see the "possibilities" and recognize your "worth" when you are surrounded by darkness. Picture a glass filled with water, a valuable resource. If the water is purified, one can easily see through it and embrace it as life-sustaining liquid. This exercise becomes a bit more difficult if the content harbors debris or what I contend are "colors" that promote an obstructed view or a decrease in value. In taking a closer look at this example as though it were a metaphor of our emotional wellbeing, I wish that you would pose two sometimes painful questions. What color is my water? What have I allowed to obstruct my view, path, and outlook?

In general, we are born with a metaphorically clear glass of water. However, our formative and adolescent years promote the intake of vast amounts of information that alter the content within our glass. We innocently receive metaphoric debris or colors with a lack of mastery for discerning good particles from bad. With untrained filters, we encounter experiences and digest information with an inability to protect ourselves from their effects. Lack of proper interventions and corrective actions can turn us into human receptacles—garbage cans—for whatever comes our way. Ironically, many of us endured this process throughout our youth, and some of us still endure this process as adults. As in our younger years, many of us have yet to master the filtering and maintenance processes of life, which allows us to discern what should be collected and purged as it relates to our glass. The mastery of this filtering process often dictates the type of self-view we hold.

As children, we were not responsible for what tainted our water. Living in a less-than-perfect family, environment, and society, we all entered adulthood with varying amounts of debris. However, as we take strides toward a greater sense of wholeness, we cannot ignore the need for a functional purification system. Partly because the negative items/perceptions in our self-view are often connected to the metaphoric debris in our glass. Hence, the value of purified versus debris-filled water becomes critical.

For all intents and purposes, the foundation of our personal out-look, esteem, and efficacy is based on the makeup of our metaphoric water. Thus, we must all strive for it to be purified and clear. In adulthood, this clarity is often determined by the ability to: 1) remove destructive colors from our glass, 2) protect our glass from the introduction of negative colors/debris, 3) ward off continuous recontamination from the same type of debris, and 4) implement behaviors that maintain purified content. This clarity promotes insight and a more authentic sense of self and personal peace. However, the lack thereof perpetuates fear, dysfunction, and turmoil.

My time volunteering with women at a Domestic Violence Shelter reinforced the value of this theory. My work there enforced the critical need for every woman to audit the colors of her past and their manifestation in her present. It taught me that each of us owe it to ourselves to be more active than passive at debilitating and removing debris to maintain content that promotes personal value, growth, and happiness. In hindsight, my work with these women started me on a journey of personal discovery from there—my own past and feelings of inadequacy—to here—a greater sense of personal empowerment and serenity.

While working with a support group there, I connected with women from many different walks of life—different ages, ethnic groups, socioeconomic backgrounds, family dynamics, and career paths. I didn't know it then, but we all had one thing in common: In many aspects of our lives, self-appreciation was a foreign concept. Though they were capable of nurturing, leading, and providing, they were strangers to the concept of self-acceptance. Tattered with bruises far beyond the physical, they were all too familiar with a diminished sense of worth and a heightened sense of powerlessness. Perpetuated over time, they developed expertise in making decisions that promoted repeated physical and emotionally destructive outcomes. Back then it amazed me to sit and listen to their stories.

Sydney was an independent and ambitious single mother when she met her husband. Feeling like she found her mate for life, she never thought abuse would be a part of her story. After the birth of her second child, simple disagreements turned to heated arguments that resulted in violence. From there, beatings and bruises were consistent and commonplace. Fearful she might lose her marriage, end up divorced like her parents, and raise two children alone, she was determined to stay. When a neighbor unexpectedly reported a domestic altercation out of fear for her safety and that of her children, she saw things further spiral out of control.

After her husband's encounter with the police, his tactics suddenly changed. First and foremost, he quit his job—refusing to look for or return to work, and was cautious to leave no visible signs of further abuse. Through intense verbal degradation, rape, and forced sleep depravation (scaring her out of her sleep by suddenly beating on objects to terrify her, forcing her to sleep on the floor or standing up against a wall) he reinforced new forms of torture, control, and imprisonment. As things got progressively worse, he started taking his anger out on their children. Only then, convinced that the lives of her children were in danger, did she decide to move to safety. By herself, she was never reason enough to leave. Like many others, Sydney didn't see herself as worthy enough to save.

For some of the women, time and circumstance left them with debris they never learned to filter. For others, the debris became a permanent identifier they assumed as part of their makeup. As a result, many of them saw themselves as worthless, and attracted people who were more than willing to reinforce that belief. Through one abusive situation after another, the colors they experienced distorted their self-view, making it increasingly difficult for them to embrace their womanhood and realize their possibilities.

In their everyday lives, many of the women covered their impurities rather well. Keeping up appearances made it easier for them to render the inner debris undetectable to the average acquaintance; however, feelings of helplessness and self-loathing would always rise to the surface when the heart was able to express itself in the surroundings of other women with the same dark secret. For many, childhood sexual abuse, violence, strained parental relationships, child maltreatment, and abandonment helped define the heaviness of their emotional baggage.

While working with this population, I connected with many women, and Maria was one who had a significant affect on me. She was a nurturer, helper, and caregiver in her profession. However, she, too, was a victim. Beneath her work uniform were countless bruises (old and new) spanning more than thirty years of abuse. Her scars stemmed from years of physical and emotional water coloring that promoted a sense of powerlessness in her situation. Perpetuated over time, the colors she received made her an expert at decisions that promoted her own demise. Back then, and now, it is difficult to understand anyone being subjected to the mutilation some of these women endured from childhood through their adult lives. Like Sydney, Maria saw herself as worthless and endured one abusive situation after another. Her experiences distorted her self-view and made it impossible for her to realize, embrace, and believe in her own possibilities.

Her high level of functioning within her job almost made it easier for her to avoid the impurities in her glass and render the debris undetectable to others. As a caregiver in the community, she covered the impurities of her content well. Though she sought to empower and be supportive to others, she often felt defeated. Childhood sexual abuse and two generations of domestic violence helped define the heaviness of her emotional baggage and threatened to irretriev- ably break her spirit. Her decision to seek help from the support group would be one of her first attempts to unlearn what she had been taught, take back her life, and learn how to live like she mattered. To do so, she would have to release the debris that plagued her adulthood with denial, victimization, and low self-esteem. Through therapy, she engaged in the ultimate fight of her life: to move beyond survival toward a sense of empowerment and freedom.

Though some of you may view the situations of these two women to be extreme and choose to shy away from how their experiences could possibly resemble your own, I pose the question again: What color is your water? As many of us suffer in silence, we endure unfulfilling relationships, harbor destructive emotional baggage, and minimize the need to care for and love ourselves. True enough, many of us have not endured the extreme treatment these women did, but on a voluntary basis we embrace situations and exhibit behaviors that disregard our worth. And, if you think none of this applies to you, look at some of the underlying beliefs that influence some of our behaviors on a regular basis. Do you recognize yourself in any of these statements?

"There's nothing truly special about me."

"If I were…then I…"

"I'm a failure."

"I'll never be…"

"I don't deserve to…"

"I'm not…"

"I can't…"

"People can't be trusted."

"I'm not good enough for…"

"I'm not worth it."

"I can't do anything right."

"I could never…"

"I'm not strong enough."

"It's my fault…"

"That could never happen for me."

Can you imagine what beliefs like these can do to influence how we see ourselves and ultimately how we move through our everyday lives? That's how powerful debris is.

With colored water and an inability to purify it, many of us have struggled to peek through darkness and grasp rays of light. We seem to fit one of three scenarios:

1. A woman whose filters are virtually inactive because she takes and keeps any debris she receives;

2. A woman whose filtering systems are intensely overworked because she frequently purifies her content but keeps allowing the same unhealthy particles into her glass time and time again;

3. A woman who is learning to master or has mastered the art of removing debris and maintaining clarity.

Which woman are you?

TRUE EMPOWERMENT WILL ONLY COME
WHEN WE ADOPT A WILLINGNESS
TO CHOOSE OURSELVES BY SEEING
OUR OWN VALUE.

If you are in the first or second group, it's time to take a serious look at the impurities that reside in your glass and ponder the question: Would any sane person drink this? As we forever pride ourselves on mastering the Art of Others, too many of us have diminished the need to master the Art of Ourselves. Think of it in terms of a newborn baby and mother relationship. What would the level of debris in your water be if you monitored your glass like a mother watching what is ingested by her newborn? As women, it's time to take this same care for ourselves.

True empowerment will only come when we adopt a willingness to choose ourselves by seeing our own value. It requires that we clearly dissect where we are, how we got there, and where we want to go. This exercise enables us to identify and label the undesirable colors that need deactivation and removal. If verbal abuse is one of your contaminating colors, it's up to you to filter it and make a conscious decision to discontinue engaging in behaviors and situations that reinforce it. This may involve engaging in therapy, support group situations, or educational opportunities that will promote your ability to make choices that filter and protect you from the destructive effects of this color. Doing so will help you: 1) define a continuum of verbal abuse extending from the subtle to more blatant forms; 2) create healthier boundaries as it relates to effective communication; and 3) engage in relationships that promote respectful conflict resolution instead of verbal intimidation, manipulation, and degradation.

Once you've filtered the contamination, the maintenance process must begin. In keeping with this example, abstain from situations that promote any level of verbal abuse would be necessary. Much like a recovered alcoholic, taking one drink after being sober cannot be safely explored. Why? The history of alcoholism and all that is connected to it makes even one drink harmful. Therefore, knowing that verbal abuse is a symbolic color of your past, part of your maintenance process would entail abstinence from communication with people who are unable to control their anger (violent communicators) or those who believe they have the right to relate to others in any inappropriate manner they choose. Being in verbally abusive situations that promote underlying beliefs like "You're stupid," "If you...Then I...," "It's all your fault", "You make me...," and "You deserve being yelled at…" are toxic. In this scenario, anything short of abstinence would threaten your goal of sustained clarity.

Nancy struggled with years of verbal abuse in her first marriage. As a teen who suffered with low self-esteem, her adulthood was plagued with the underlying belief that she always did and said things that brought out the worst in the men she loved. In a vicious cycle passed down from her father, being part of a verbally abusive relationship served to reinforce her already poor self-view. When her marriage ended, she was devastated. As she sought to get back on her feet, she saw how powerful and dominant negative communication had been throughout her entire development. Identifying and removing the debris of other people's words, judgments, and cruelty became critical to her filtering process.

Through therapy, she confronted painful encounters and gained insight that helped repair her esteem and facilitate the move toward personal restoration and renewal. When she started to reevaluate her personal and professional relationships, her expectations changed. Having worked to resolve and filter her contamination, she embraced the value of positive communication and reciprocation as appropriate expectations. Not only did she gain the skills and courage needed to express herself, but she no longer accepted others disregarding or belittling her views as the norm. Across the board, she categorized those that were unable to respectfully and constructively engage in conversation, feedback, and conflict as unhealthy and threatening to her new sense of self-respect. Regard for the woman who could now see the good in herself was paramount.

———————————— • ▬ • ————————————

RECEIVING ACCOLADES FOR TAKING CARE OF "HIM," "HER," "IT," AND "THEM" IS TO BE CELEBRATED, BUT THIS IS NOT A PERMISSION SLIP TO IGNORE THE NEED TO VALUE AND TAKE CARE OF "YOU."

———————————— • ▬ • ————————————

As you engage in this process, you will see how critical toxicity is to defining how we feel about ourselves. Receiving accolades for taking care of "him," "her," "it," and "them" is to be celebrated, but this is not a permission slip to ignore the need to value and take care of "you." Starting today, dealing with ourselves on a reactive versus proactive basis is no longer acceptable. It's not enough to look in the mirror only to put something on or take something off your face. How about seeing the woman behind the face? Can you connect with the woman in your reflection?

When you take a real look at the woman in the mirror, what do you see? What do you really, truly think of her? As you read the first item of the Insight Corner for this chapter, I want you to place your name on the line given before the words "Self-View" (for example, mine would read "Nicole's Self-View"). This exercise is critical. With no thoughts about how you would like to see yourself or how you want people to see you, place a word on each line that describes how you truly view yourself now. Don't censure; just write what you feel—the good, bad, ugly, and indifferent. Don't shy away from the truth, even if it calls up words like unlovable, scared, fearful, loser, loving, ashamed, angry, powerful, judgmental, stupid, intelligent, kind, failure, or achiever, to name a few. Whatever words you come up with, whether positive, negative, or a mix of both, they must be a true assessment of how you really feel about yourself. Don't analyze or over-think this; just let your heart guide the expression of your truth. As you embark on completing this chapter's Insight Corner, be prepared to take the blinders off and take a courageous first step in a process that's customized and all your own. May an authentic look at your self-view lend new insight and propel your journey to the next chapter.

Seven Critical Reminders for Your Journey Forward

- You already have what you need to achieve a true sense of happiness. You have more inside than you give yourself credit for—stop looking outside of yourself to find what is already located within.

- Your true power will only be realized when you embrace a willingness to choose yourself by seeing your own value. Make the connection: How you feel about yourself is a major factor in how you're experiencing your life.

- It's not enough to just look in the mirror; it's about connecting with the woman in your reflection and celebrating the woman behind the face.

- Your personal outlook, esteem, and ability to accomplish results is significantly influenced by the debris in your water and the negativity in your underlying beliefs. Fortunately, you have what it takes to master the filtering process and discern what should be kept and what should be purged.

- When your self-view is negative and distorted it is increasingly difficult to realize your possibilities. You owe it to yourself to be more active at developing and maintaining content that promotes versus diminishes your infinite value, growth, and happiness.

- Disregarding yourself is not an access pass to womanhood. Valuing your spiritual, emotional, and physical health is not just a priority but a birthright you must revere and hold sacred.

- Embracing the journey of personal discovery from your own feelings of self-deficiency to a sense of peace and empowerment is critical to finding the woman you were born to be.

INSIGHT CORNER

1. Clearing any thoughts about how you would like to see yourself or be seen by others, place your name inside the circle and place a word on each line that describes how you truly view yourself. Don't censor; just let the illustration capture the truth.

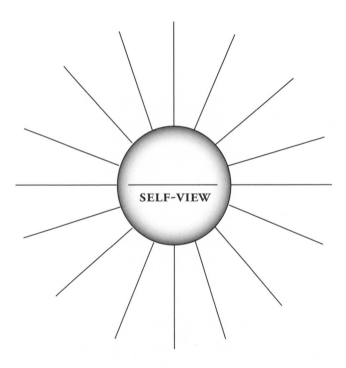

SELF-VIEW

2. What do you consider to be some of the negative underlying beliefs that drive how you move through your everyday life?

_____

_____

_____

_____

3. How would you experience your life if you no longer held on to the negative items expressed in the illustration of your self-view?

_____

_____

_____

_____

4. What are some of the negative things that serve to pollute your water?

_____

_____

_____

_____

5. What do you perceive to be the connection between the negative items in your self-view diagram and the contaminants that have served to taint your water? For example, you might have the word "unattractive" on your self-view and some of what you may identify as contaminants feeding into this self-view may be: being singled out as a child for the way you looked, rarely being validated by your parents, being asked to change your appearance by people you were romantically involved with, etc.

_____

_____

_____

_____

6. What can you do to purify your content and eliminate the effects of your negative/contaminating colors?

_____

_____

_____

_____

7. What are at least five things you can use as an action plan to protect yourself from future contamination?

_____

_____

_____

_____

8. Who can you ask to be your accountability partner in moving forward an action plan to protect yourself from future contamination?

_____

_____

Chapter 2:

WHAT IS GOD'S VIEW OF YOU?

EVERY TIME WE EAT AWAY AT
OUR OWN WORTH, WE JEOPARDIZE
MOVING WITHIN THE PURPOSE FOR
WHICH WE WERE CREATED.

AS WOMEN, WE ARE in a great battle concerning society's standards of beauty, womanhood, and worth. It's hard to maintain a positive self-view under these circumstances. Every time we eat away at our own worth, we jeopardize moving within the purpose for which we were created. We must seriously evaluate the template we use to define our value. How accurate is that standard? We all appear to have bought into some level of defining ourselves by trends, friends, television, and the like. Maybe that's why holding onto a negative self-view is so easy. From childhood to adulthood, many of us have adopted a self-view that is less than celebratory and often debilitating. Yet a positive and authentic self-view is the way to happiness. Herein lies the question: If happiness begins from within, how do we get started? Whose view can we trust as a template for our intrinsic worth?

As a life and executive coach, I am charged with promoting the achievement of personal and professional goals in the lives of my clients. In my experience, the self-view of a client often serves to promote or challenge his or her success. In every case, it becomes a key contributor in how the client approaches the coaching process. In this role, I have the pleasure of encouraging and strategizing with both women and men as they journey toward their personal and career achievements. Though they're all very different, they continuously reinforce how similar we all are as human beings. With varying personalities, views of the world, value systems, religious affiliations, and personal experiences they enforce the undeniable criticality of a positive self-view. Never was this point more evident than when I worked with Laurie.

I worked with Laurie for about three sessions when an unexpected opportunity for change presented itself. She was a successful business-woman with vast public accolades, yet she was struggling with doubt as it related to her leadership capabilities. While we were together, she expressed her insecurities concerning the expansion of her role as an executive. Though the conversation centered around competencies, scope of influence, and sharpening her leadership skills, the greatest challenge appeared to surround the critical distortions in her self-view.

As she shared some of her personal apprehensions, an exercise occurred to me that I believe came as a divine instruction; following this directive, I took out a sheet of paper. On the sheet, I drew a sun with rays, much like the one you filled out at the end of chapter one. If you didn't complete that exercise, stop here. It's critical that you go back and do that before you continue reading. Once I drew it, I put her name in the middle with the words "self-view" under it and asked that she afford herself permission to be vulnerable and honest at all costs. I asked that she give me an outward expression of words that described how she saw herself. With great courage, she obliged my request. When the exercise was complete, the words drew a picture that screamed volumes. The numerous negative and critical things she held as part of her self-view clearly displayed she was unable, in that moment, to give herself the credit God had already bestowed upon her.

After moving that illustration aside, I did something I had never done before: I took out a second sheet of paper and though I drew the same illustration, this time I gave it a different title. Instead of Laurie's name and the word "Self-View," I placed the words "God-View" in the center. Without knowing how she would respond, I then asked her to list some adjectives that could describe how God saw her.

To my surprise, the words came like a flood. One after the other, they just kept on coming. And they were vastly different from the words she gave for her self-view. All of the words listed in her God-view were positive, empowering, and affirming, every last one of them. Through and through her God-view exuded possibility, value, owner-ship, and strength. Recognizing that negative attributes were not of God, it was as if she knew God saw her as fearfully and wonderfully made. Once completed, we placed both views side by side. As we com-pared the illustrations, I asked what would happen if she saw herself the way she perceived God did? What would happen if she approached her goals through her God-view verses her self-view? What if she accepted her negative self-view as a distortion—a lie? A lie that was distracting her from the truth of her inner brilliance. A lie that was meant to keep her in a battle with her feelings of self-doubt. In that meeting, Laurie grasped the idea that her God-view was limitless and truthful while her negative self-view was limiting and deceiving. At this point, I asked her what would happen if she afforded the adoption of her God-view to replace her self-view, and she answered, "That would change everything." In that moment, I saw her turn a corner.

Through this exercise, Laurie found the courage to go back to the power of her God-given definition—her true beginning—and embrace her right to ask the question: What did she really want for her life and how could God use her to be a light for others? With her cup running over, she spoke with clarity, devoid of apology, fear, or worthlessness. Discarding a self-view that promoted insecurity, she held tight to an illustration that represented a snapshot of personal freedom, authority, and hope. Doing so, she was able to embrace her God-view as her clear glass of water. By opening up to a spirit greater than herself, she got a glimpse of how great she was to God and how much greater she needed to be to herself.

I've done this exercise with just about every client since and the results have all been the same—life changing. No matter what religious affiliation or level of spirituality, the exercise has opened the opportunity for each client to embrace his or her true power. Each has created a powerful picture to illustrate a greatness that would yield a God-given purpose. From it, they see how such greatness can make a difference in the world.

Paula was no different. When I met her, she was truly a force to be reckoned with. A public figure and respected activist, she fought tirelessly to hide her struggle with drug addiction for over twenty years. Using drugs to numb her personal pain and feelings of resentment, she was emotionally withdrawn from many of the significant moments of her life. Throughout most of her life, she was able to avoid and deny the effect her choices had on everyone around her. In all her years of addiction, she never made a serious and successful attempt at sobriety. In fact, her adamant refusal for help made those who loved her feel that her drug problem might never be one that she would overcome.

When I sat down with her to draw her self-view, the illustration revealed a portrait that was laden with guilt, sadness, regret, and despair. Though it was painful, she looked at the illustration and confronted the depiction of who she thought she really was. In that moment, it became obvious that her self-view was the affliction and her addiction presented itself as a cure. When first asked about her God-view, she was overwhelmed and distraught. So much so that she felt unworthy of contemplating how God saw her. I soon learned this was a question that lay heavy on her heart. As we moved through documenting her God-view, a new option, slowly presented itself—an option that had no hidden agenda. It was not based on what others wanted from her, thought of her, or expected of her life.

She was able to declare her God-view based on her embrace of God's unwavering love. Through words of truth, it became clear that God was bigger than her choices, disappointments, and decisions. I remember telling her nothing could redefine what God originally defined, because God was deliberate in designing every creation. In other words, whatever she thought of herself, if it wasn't in line with God's view of her, was a flawed impersonation. The woman she was born to be, the woman God created her to be was ever present, whether or not she chose to believe it, own it, or feel worthy of it. Therefore, what God defined in her, no one, not even she had the power to redefine. The idea that God didn't define her worth by anything other than how she was initially created was the breakthrough that placed her on a freeing journey from self-destruction.

Paula's God-view was the one definition she hadn't been able to envision. She had no frame of reference for it, so it was easy to see why she couldn't get to it when she needed it most. This newfound clarity served to make sense of the utter chaos in her life. For Paula, this was the authentic definition of who she was despite what she had or hadn't done. It was the light needed to help her move beyond what had become her life.

By placing affirmative and positive attributes in the position of power over the negative and deficient ones, the greatness afforded by God is positioned as the foundation of your true existence.

Shortly after, for the first time in decades, Paula did the unexpected. She made the decision to journey toward sobriety. Now, when she felt unworthy she could stand on the recognition that she didn't have the power to redefine greatness, leaving her with two choices: fail to try or stand in the definition that was assigned by God and refuse to give up. As she took the plunge into the unknown aspects of the rehabilitation process, her God-view illustration served as a courageous, powerful, and truthful depiction of who she really was. Now, she is taking the journey of sobriety one day at a time, successfully working through her challenges, and seeking to walk in God's purpose for her life one day at a time.

For Paula and many others, this exercise broke down walls and spoke to a predestined greatness. By placing affirmative and positive attributes in the position of power over the negative and deficient ones, the greatness afforded by God is positioned as the foundation of your true existence.

For example, most chefs would agree fresh ingredients make the best dishes. A culinary masterpiece starts with having a great foundation from which to create great cuisine. As I relayed to one client, God is the beginning and the end, so when we connect to that truth, it becomes much easier to recognize that most of the problem is in the middle. We move off the course of our divine direction when our self-view is out of line with where we must begin, our God-view. In the middle is where we dismiss God's intention for our lives, doubt our ability to live up to our full potential, and let others sell us on the concept that we are powerless instead of powerful beyond measure. This can significantly shift and complicate the navigation of our journey. For many, the middle prompts faulty thinking that is diametrically opposed to the greatness God sees in each of us.

If you don't go back to the beginning, the journey from great to greatness becomes a spiritual battle that is often controlled by what you think. When you are able to internalize and have a clear view of God's adoration for you, the negative aspects of our self-view become minimized and living in the image you were created to manifest takes precedent. When this happens and we embrace a self-view that is a close reflective image of our God-view, what we strive for is no longer beyond our reach, what we can accomplish is no longer out of the scope of possibility, and the difference we can make in the lives of others is no longer minimized. The inappropriate self-talk, actions, and limitations are no longer effective tools to keep us from seeing who we were made to be. If we can focus on the beginning and use that illustration as evidence of our own personal masterpiece, we have no choice but to move through our lives differently.

WHEN YOU ARE ABLE TO INTERNALIZE AND HAVE A CLEAR VIEW OF GOD'S ADORATION FOR YOU, THE NEGATIVE ASPECTS OF OUR SELF-VIEW BECOME MINIMIZED AND LIVING IN THE IMAGE YOU WERE CREATED TO MANIFEST TAKES PRECEDENT.

When I tried the exercise for myself, it quickly became apparent that I, too, was challenged to see beyond my perceived inadequacies. Being open to the process, I embraced a greater sense of personal clarity toward purpose, living, and loving. Like my clients, comparing my self-view and God-view gave me a visual understanding of why one view presented obstacles in moving forward whereas the other expected forward movement as the only natural progression. As a child of God, my God-view was a reflection of goodness and abundance. Thankfully, I was nowhere near the self-view I held five years earlier. When I compared my recent self-view (e.g., including the words influential, powerful, loved, leader, compassionate, fun, giving, creative, change agent, intelligent) and past self-view (e.g., including the words ashamed, unworthy, angry, hurt, unloved, failure, and not good enough) I could really see the utility of this exercise.

When I took note of my past self-view compared to the self-view I held while doing the exercise, there was a critically vast difference. Though I still had room to grow, looking at my past self-view and my present self-view was like looking at two different people. Though I didn't have the name "God-view" for it then, the embrace of my worth would be the significant difference between both periods in my life. Reflecting back, I could see how many barriers were lifted, and I could also embrace the significance of blessings and opportunities that came into my life as a result of the change in my self-view. The significant change in how I lived my life when my self-view was light years away from my God-view could not be ignored.

For my clients and myself, embracing our God-view on a daily basis has become a personal mandate. Seeking to internalize the descriptions in their illustrations, many have turned their God-view into usable graphics that affirm who they are and who they've always been. Some have duplicated it to hang on their walls and stick on their mirrors, while others have pasted it on their treadmills, turned it into bookmarks, and chose to use it as screen savers, all in an attempt to remind themselves of a more powerful and authentic view of who they really are.

WHEN YOU LOOK AT YOUR
GOD-VIEW IT WILL BECOME
APPARENT THAT CERTAIN PHRASES LIKE
"I CAN'T" AND "I COULD NEVER"
DON'T BELONG ANYMORE.

Now, I ask the same question of you: How does God view you? Without imposing your own view of yourself, dare to complete your God-view illustration in the Insight Corner. Once you do, you should memorize it, own it, repeat it, and find ways to live it in your everyday life. When you look at your God-view it will become apparent that certain phrases like "I can't" and "I could never" don't belong anymore. Instead, "I can" and "I will" will be assessed as a more appropriate fit.

Seven Critical Reminders for Your Journey Forward

- As a child of God, your God-view is the true depiction of your intrinsic worth.

- Your God-view can be trusted as an authentic view of the woman you were born to be. It is positive, empowering, and affirming. Not only does it exude possibility and strength, but it is a reflection of your goodness and true abundance.

- God didn't define your worth by anything other than how you were initially created, so it's time to push beyond your self-doubt. God sees beyond your past choices and perceived failures, so your permission to be brilliant has been permanently granted.

- Paying attention to other people's definition of you and adopting a self-view that is less than celebratory distracts you from the truth of your inner greatness. Remember, your God-view is limitless whereas a negative self-view is limiting.

- Every time you eat away at your own worth you jeopardize moving within the purpose for which God created you. With your God-view, striving for what you want, taking charge of your life, and fulfilling your personal purpose becomes a natural progression.

- Be willing to open up to a spirit greater than yourself, see how great you are to God, and how much greater you need to be to yourself. Devoid of apology and fear, embrace your freedom, authority, and divine destination.

- You have the right to declare what you want for your life and God's glory.

INSIGHT CORNER

1. As a child of God, how does God view you?

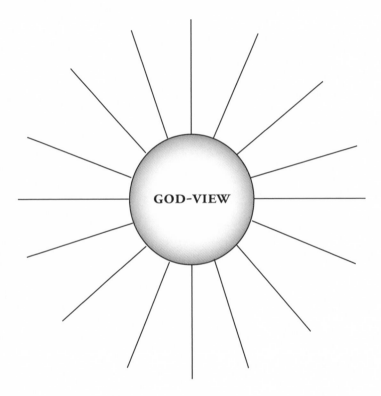

GOD-VIEW

2. Looking at both illustrations (your God-view and your self-view), can you see how one limits and the other liberates? What would happen if you saw yourself the way you perceived God to see you?

_____

_____

_____

_____

3. What does your God-view say you can accomplish that your self-view says you can't?

_____

_____

_____

_____

4. What would happen if you approached life, living, and purpose through your God-view? How much easier would it be to define what you want and feel deserving of your purpose through your God-view versus any negativity stated in your self-view?

_____

_____

_____

_____

TAKE CHARGE OF
YOUR PAST

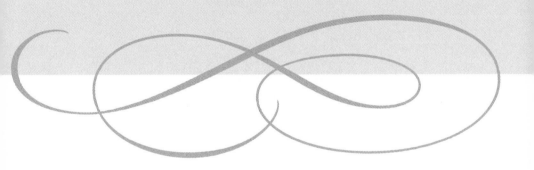

Chapter 3:

LET GO OF THE HEAVY CARGO, START TO TRAVEL LIGHT

AS WE THINK OF OUR WOMANLY journey toward peace, balance, and purpose, we often struggle with the recognition that an overloaded spirit cannot travel at optimum efficiency. Despite this reality, time and circumstance often promote our tendency toward traveling heavy instead of traveling light. When I first went on vacation with my husband, I remember how stunned he was that I packed two large suitcases and one duffel bag to his one piece of carry-on luggage. We were both going to the same place and staying the same amount of time, but I needed to carry everything I could think of—just in case. Like my overpacked luggage, many of us collect people, places, and things that represent quantity rather than quality in our lives. Instead of choosing ourselves and traveling light, many of us struggle with fear of loss and perceptions of permanence that serve to further weigh us down.

Like moving to a new apartment or home, everything in your current residence should not be moved to the next location. Some things need to be disposed of, given away, or simply left behind. As you pack boxes for the transition, its up to you to evaluate each object's importance as it relates to your new home. This process offers an exercise in removal versus accumulation. For many of us, packing offers a needed opportunity to assess the value and utility of items acquired throughout the years. This effort helps to identify items that have claimed space because of past need rather than present usefulness. However, the logical nature of this process does not eliminate the battle between what should stay and what should go.

FOR MANY OF US, PACKING OFFERS A NEEDED OPPORTUNITY TO ASSESS THE VALUE AND UTILITY OF ITEMS ACQUIRED THROUGHOUT THE YEARS. THIS EFFORT HELPS TO IDENTIFY ITEMS THAT HAVE CLAIMED SPACE BECAUSE OF PAST NEED RATHER THAN PRESENT USEFULNESS.

For example, there are at least fifteen pairs of shoes I own but never wear, yet I can't seem to bring myself to give them away. These shoes have graced my closet for such a long time that most have become permanent fixtures. When I purchased each pair, I justified their ownership, but as time passed, my inability to use them did not prompt getting rid of them. I mean, what would I do if they were gone? What would I do if I needed them for a future event?

As we move toward embracing the premise of living fully, the word *change* becomes inescapable. Despite our need for familiarity, each metaphoric move from one place to another screams that a transformation is necessary. Sometimes the move requires that we alter our perceptions, expectations, and even attitudes. In general, living like you matter requires a continuous clean-up of life space. It imparts an individual responsibility to seek and surround yourself with people, places, and things that work to reinforce your sense of personal empowerment, fulfillment, and purpose. In so doing, we must recognize, challenge, and eliminate elements that occupy our lives because of time spent, familiarity, or worse yet, fear. Without this process, the accumulation of dead weight becomes inevitable.

This dead weight is counterproductive at best. For example, think of yourself on a rowboat carrying 250 pounds of useless cargo. All things being equal, you could almost guarantee that this type of cargo would promote a strenuous, if not seemingly impossible, journey. In theory, throwing the items overboard would be a simple solution. However, losing weight is never easy. Freedom from unproductive relationships, jobs, criticism, and experiences that weigh us down is no simple task.

In the midst of a personal and professional world wind, Terri was unprepared when she realized she had to cut the deadweight from her life. What was once a meeting of the minds and the creation of a promising entrepreneurial venture had now become a business partnership that represented a financial and emotional nightmare. Entangled in a very stressful dynamic, Terri admitted that she should have been more cautious in making the decision to enter the partnership to begin with. In being more focused on the viability of the business idea than of the person she was going into business with, she opened the door to disaster.

From the beginning, her partner showed warning signs of potential trouble (credit issues and an inability to secure financing). However, creative explanations of why her financial history presented the way it did, coupled with Terri's blind allegiance and fear of confrontation, kept things moving forward. As the business relationship progressed, she found that her partner's financial circumstances were only matched by her questionable business practices and lack of relational integrity. The more Terri sought to justify that it was cheaper to work through her partner's poor decisions and shortcomings, the more she avoided how much the relationship was weighing her down by violating her own value system.

Over time, casual conversation turned into platforms for dreaded arguments and disrespectful communication. For Terri, the decision to travel light would require a change in her business dealings. Though she hated to admit it, part of her hesitation was based on feeling as though she failed at what she once believed was a foolproof idea and relationship. When she took a true cost/benefit analysis of her situation, the costs outweighed the benefits of holding onto her partnership. The operational, emotional, and physical costs, not to mention the years spent, presented a clear view of why she had now arrived at a potential breaking point. As a result, she formulated an action plan to exit from the business. As she phased out of the partnership, she used the experiences learned, her strong business relationships, and her new-found perspective to start her own company and be in control of her career on her own terms.

For Terri, it took courage to identify the dead weight of the relationship and even more courage when she made the decision to distance herself from it. Living like we matter requires that we stop and acknowledge the need to shed excess weight, or at minimum, render it powerless. Allowing people and things to coexist with you, despite the ill effects on your personal growth and happiness, is not healthy. If something consistently puts you in a negative space, or someone is rarely positive, selfless, or constructive toward you, it's time to make a change. It's time to start traveling light. In doing so, you make a giant step in taking responsibility for your own sense of wholeness and well-being.

For each of us, traveling light suggests that nothing and no one be allowed to be in your life for the sheer purpose of occupancy.

For each of us, traveling light suggests that nothing and no one be allowed to be in your life for the sheer purpose of occupancy. If you don't ascribe to this, you go against the notion that you deserve to surround yourself with people, places, and things that are good to and for you. In essence, everyone and everything should earn its space. Even a family pet earns its keep through promoting joy, laughter, and companionship. If this seems selfish, think again. Simply put, anything else equates to less than you deserve.

As women, recognizing what we don't need is critical. We cannot afford occupancy that unnecessarily weighs us down. Not only does it lead to the promotion of stress, anxiety, exhaustion, and low self-esteem but it serves to overshadow and influence the very nature of personal wholeness. Why? Because the excess, occupies space that would normally be used more efficiently. As we venture to make a shift, we must acknowledge five simple truths that serve to solidify our commitment to traveling light:

- People's actions speak a greater truth than their words, so we should pay attention to what they do instead of what they say.
- Our gut instinct deserves to be listened to and highly revered instead of being second guessed and ignored.
- We have the right to protect our time and choose to spend it with people who appreciate and respect it.
- Anyone or anything that creates more discomfort and sadness than joy needs to be removed.
- The wholeness of who you are is not defined by anyone else; it's only defined by you and God.

The avoidance of these truths often aids in justifying and prolonging the unnecessary loads many of us continue to carry. For example, it is not unusual to cling to people's words and ignore their actions. As some of us struggle with fears of being judged, wronged, or misunderstood, we simply ignore what people's actions tell us.

When Cheryl's boyfriend told her she was being ridiculous for questioning changes in his behavior, she chose to believe his words over his actions. Despite her gut instinct, a poorly explained explicit e-mail to another woman, a reduction in his free time, and a subtle request to no longer answer his cell phone, she chose to go against her first thoughts and convince herself there was no cause for concern.

On the night she decided to catch up with an old girlfriend, she passed by an unfamiliar home and recognized his car in the driveway. When she asked him of his whereabouts he told her he was having a drink with some of his colleagues from work. Later, she confirmed the home was that of an ex-girlfriend but chose to give him the benefit of the doubt. When she finally brought up the young lady's name in a conversation, he defensively denied having any communication with her. Hurt and dismayed, she alerted him to the fact that she was sitting outside of the residence looking at the license plate on the back of his car on the night in question. Caught, he immediately became agitated and threatened to break up with her if she chose not to trust him. Fortunately, she chose to keep him accountable to his actions instead of his words. Seeking to learn from lessons of the past, she was determined to assert that she mattered enough to be in a honest situation and decided to break off the relationship. Soon after, she confirmed that she did indeed make the right decision when she saw him and the young lady out together.

Cheryl's situation begs the question: What is wrong with holding a person accountable for their actions despite what they tell you? A person who says what they've done, what they're doing, or what they're going to do and does something different is giving you a first sign that something may not be what it seems. A person who does what they say they will, or is seen to keep their word, is usually considered to be a person of integrity. So, why not trust a person's actions? Contrary to popular belief, mature and responsible adults don't need us to make excuses for them. Just as we are expected to be responsible for our actions, we must learn to feel comfortable with accepting the same standard of others.

We must also be willing to listen to our gut instinct. As you saw in Cheryl's scenario, instinct is critical because it will often tell us whether or not the person deserves the benefit of the doubt. Unfortunately, many of us ignore glaring red lights, in favor of pretending they are green. Our gut instinct may say "stop," "wait," or "use caution," yet we keep right on going full speed ahead.

I once had a job interview with a manager who gave me a really bad feeling. His body language and conversation had a very insecure, tense tone. I drove home thinking, "I'm not so sure about this." However, I convinced myself that I was being ridiculous and accepted the position when it was offered. From the first day of employment to the last, my gut instinct was affirmed. The anger and frustration I experienced proved I should have left the interview and run as far away from that job as I could. But I didn't respect my instinct enough to accept what it was saying. The price I paid for that decision was my own peace of mind.

A couple of years later a similar scenario occurred, but this time I listened. Though initially excited about a leadership position at a major corporation, I refused to accept a third interview when my instincts screamed that the situation would be a demanding and chaotic distraction from my path of purpose. This time around, I could not let the salary, title, or promise of career advancement persuade me when my gut was telling me the opportunity was not the right one for me. This time, my intuition was telling me to stop, and I listened to it. Looking back, I know I made the right decision. The day after I declined, I took my first trip to Starbucks and started writing the book you now hold in your hands. I took a chance, listened to my heart, and created what is now Volition Enterprises, Inc., a personal and professional development corporation that helps people and companies reach their full potential.

IN ADDITION TO IGNORING OUR INTUITION, MANY OF US RETAIN RELATIONSHIPS WITH PEOPLE WHO ARE BONA FIDE TAKERS.

In addition to ignoring our intuition, many of us retain relationships with people who are bona fide takers. These people rarely give and often suck the energy out of most people with whom they come in contact. Yet we symbolically choose them over ourselves when we choose to keep them around. And, denial does not change the fact that these people fit in the dead weight category perfectly. When we allow them to be an intricate part of our lives, they often promote feelings of deficiency rather than rejuvenation. Like bank accounts, we become unbalanced when there are steady withdrawals without deposits.

Harboring these people in our lives is just as burdensome as defining who we are by using the standards of others. Isn't seeking to live up to your own standards and those of God enough? You are the only *person* who needs to define you. It is your job to see yourself as a vessel of hope, possibility, and greatness. Self-definition is a power that you own unless you accept the dead weight of letting others run your life. If we let go of what others think, we are able to hear our own God-given thoughts more clearly. It's no longer worth it to eliminate healthy standards and expectations (such as respect, honesty, reciprocation, compromise, and effective communication) just to keep someone around.

YOU ARE THE ONLY *PERSON* WHO NEEDS
TO DEFINE YOU. IT IS YOUR JOB TO SEE
YOURSELF AS A VESSEL OF HOPE,
POSSIBILITY, AND GREATNESS.

It's time to throw the cargo overboard! You may decide to walk away or just admit the truth, but action is most definitely required. As you embrace the loss of deadweight, you'll find that doing so embraces what I call the Muscle Challenge: a conscious decision to seek and retain fruitful friendships; revere one's gut instinct; work within equally yoked and compatible romantic relationships; spend time based on personal choice; and surround oneself with resources, people, and things that promote personal development and enhancement. For the most part, you'll build muscle rather quickly on this journey, but don't get discouraged by the items that may take a bit more time, planning, and execution to yield the results you want. For example, Tara was a first-time college student at the age of thirty-one when we met. Her decision to pursue her education was an attempt to lose the dead weight of an unfulfilling job and gain the muscle of financial flexibility and fulfillment within a new career. Although in the interim her decision to obtain a college degree was challenging, the long term effort was necessary to release the weight that was hindering her personal growth. Though her degree would not be achieved overnight, her combined commitment and effort would be a conscious decision to lose the weight and inadvertently move toward gaining muscle.

As in Tara's scenario, muscle is the best replacement for dead weight because it creates a stronger sense of self. It works for you, rather than against you. It builds endurance and confidence while promoting the use of tools like honesty, determination, and integrity to maintain a sense of personal liberation. Building muscle is a celebration of the five truths of traveling light. So, if you question what you will do when the dead weight is gone, my answer is, you'll finally start to live. Remember, clutter has never afforded much room for openings or opportunities. No matter how you slice it, dead weight is a liability. The decision to perceive the release of it as an opportunity to spread your wings and live a more content and fulfilling life is a choice—one only you can make.

IF YOU QUESTION WHAT YOU WILL DO
WHEN THE DEAD WEIGHT IS GONE, MY
ANSWER IS, YOU'LL FINALLY START TO LIVE.

SEVEN CRITICAL REMINDERS FOR YOUR JOURNEY FORWARD

- An overloaded spirit cannot travel at optimum efficiency; building muscle is the way to go.

- As you move toward the premise of whole living, the word "change" becomes inescapable. Each metaphoric move from one place to another will require a transformation and a definite shift in your perceptions, expectations, and attitude.

- Nothing and no one should be allowed in your life for the sheer purpose of occupancy. Everyone and everything should earn its space.

- It's your prerogative to eliminate elements that merely occupy your life because of time spent, familiarity, or fear. Without this process, the accumulation of dead weight is inevitable.

- Ignoring the reality that dead weight is harmful does not make it harmless. No matter how you slice it, dead weight is a liability.

- Dare to embrace and start using the five simple truths of traveling light: 1) Pay attention to what people do versus what they say; 2) Listen to and regard your gut instinct as a protective blessing; 3) Be a good manager of your time and require that others do the same; 4) Rid yourself of anyone or anything that creates more sadness than joy; and 5) Remember, the wholeness of who you are is only defined by you and God, no one else.

- It's no longer worth it to eliminate healthy standards and expectations (such as respect, honesty, reciprocation, compromise, and effective communication) just to keep someone around. Dare to throw the cargo overboard and embrace the Muscle Challenge.

INSIGHT CORNER

1. Who and what can be characterized as dead weight in your life?

_____

_____

_____

_____

2. Why do you consider those items to be dead weight?

_____

_____

_____

_____

3. Why do you think you hold onto the weight that you've identified?

_____

_____

_____

_____

4. What would happen if you decided to remove the dead weight from your life?

_____

_____

_____

_____

5. What will you do to remove or minimize the dead weight?

_____

_____

_____

_____

6. When will you start the removal process?

_____

_____

a. How will you do it, what actions will you execute?

_____

_____

_____

_____

b. How will you keep yourself accountable to your action plan?

_____

_____

_____

_____

7. Once the dead weight is removed, how will you build muscle in your life?

_____

_____

_____

a. What new or unused resources will you tap into?

_____

_____

_____

_____

b. With what type of people or places will you seek to surround yourself?

_____

_____

_____

_____

c. What new opportunities/activities will you embrace?

_____

_____

_____

_____

Chapter 4:

IT'S TIME TO TAKE DOMINION

IN MANY CULTURES, THE WORD *dominion* is defined as the power to direct, control, use, and dispose of. Simply, it refers to the principle of authority. The word *dominion* in conjunction with the phrase *"moment of impact"* can be quite meaningful to the premise of wholeness. In general, a moment of impact is often defined as an action or event that makes an impression due to its timing, context, or delivery. One example of a moment of impact might be a new CEO announcing the adoption of an open-door policy and collaborative approach to business at a historically cut-throat and internally competitive company while onlookers simultaneously witness each executive's office door being unhinged and removed by the company's maintenance crew. In this incident, the doors being unscrewed from their frames and removed from the building in conjunction with the announcement of a new work environment would be considered a moment of impact. Its timing, delivery, and context automatically affected those who witnessed the event. With deliberate and strategic intent, the CEO sought to gain everyone's attention by introducing information in a manner few would forget.

For obvious reasons, this impersonal event is not as emotionally laden as a personal one, however, personal ones are often more extreme. They have no middle ground—they are either very positive or very negative. For example, the day a woman is proposed to by the one she loves represents a positive moment of impact. When positive, they serve to boost your esteem and create a sense of contentment. When negative, they can be traumatic, debilitating, and haunting. One easily calls for celebration, whereas the other desperately calls for dominion.

On December 21, 1988 my aunt received the call that pulled life's rug right out from under her. A terrorist bomb had exploded aboard Pan Am flight 103 over Lockerbie, Scotland, killing 270 passengers and crew. One of those passengers was her beloved husband and the father of their then eleven-year-old son. The pain of this loss resounded through every member of the family and to millions across the globe. A good husband and father, he was on his way home for the holidays. A respected wife and mother, she had no idea she was preparing for an arrival that would never happen. As his wife, it was a tragic moment of impact she will forever remember. As his niece, it was a tragic moment of impact I will never forget.

In a split second, moments like these can change your outlook on life. In some instances, they can emotionally victimize over and over, thus sustaining their effect for long periods. For some, these events can become frozen situations unaffected by time and place. In this context, time may not promote a significant enough diminishing effect. Instead, it may cultivate a mastery of avoidance, suppression, and denial. Whether a five-year-old girl or a woman of fifty, the power of these events to re-victimize or bring forth feelings of inadequacy, sorrow, and fear remain relative. For this reason, people often become imprisoned by their own moments of personal impact. As a prisoner, one is often controlled by the event in some way. This state of imprisonment can only be fought through the decision to move toward dominion and authority. The primary defense against permanent emotional scarring and prolonged devastation is the quest for dominion. In its essence, it requires a willingness to acknowledge our feelings (e.g., vulnerability, betrayal, violation) so we can take authority over the effects.

As a personal survivor of abuse, I know that the trip to authority over these experiences is not on the "best place to vacation" list. Sexually molested at the age of five by my step-grandfather, early childhood was quite confusing for me. I battled feeling isolated, dirty, and unlovable as a result of his perversion. Bound to secrecy by my own fear I maintained my silence until I was almost 19 years old. I reached my breaking point on the eve of his death when my mother declared her intention to help plan and pay for his funeral proceedings. Not knowing he had violated her most sacred trust, I felt victimized all over again. Desperate, distraught, and dying inside, I reached out for help. That week, I entered into therapy. Having come to the end of my rope, my journey toward owning my feelings initiated my own personal quest for dominion. Confronting feelings of guilt, betrayal, helplessness, and anger, was just the beginning. I had long suppressed the fact that I felt my innocence was robbed and my spirit was left for dead. Most painfully, I had to own my personal truth: Through the actions of a child predator disguised as a loving relative, my body and spirit were brutally violated.

EVERY TIME I HID FROM MY EMOTIONAL WOUNDS AND DENOUNCED MY NEED FOR HEALING, I MADE THE INCIDENTS MORE POWERFUL THAN MYSELF.

As a survivor of sexual abuse, the process of trying to take authority over an event that happened more than fifteen years prior was extremely difficult. Recognizing I still felt pain over the situation though so much time had passed, made me feel more weak and vulnerable. Making the conscious decision to move beyond faking that "everything in my life was great," I had to stop avoiding certain conversations, feelings, childhood memories, and people. In other words, my break came from being tired of feeling terrorized. Most of all, I was tired of terrorizing myself. Every time I hid from my emotional wounds and denounced my need for healing, I made the incident more powerful than myself. I went from childhood through young adulthood before recognizing the need for dominion. After two years of working to achieve it, I took the courageous step of disclosing my pain to my family.

For the most part, the quest for dominion is never an overnight process. Therefore, it especially interests me when I hear women say things like, "It happened and I'm over it." My consistent reaction of disbelief comes from the notion that you don't just "get over it." Hence, I find the purpose of this statement to be one of convincing ourselves rather than the people to whom we proclaim it. In fact, I don't know that one ever "gets over" certain moments of impact. You can render it powerless over your emotions, behaviors, and decisions, but you don't just delete and forget it.

For many of us, negative moments of impact become life-altering events long after they happen. Some of us have tried to ignore them, but the more you do, the more they have a way of residing in your subconscious and manifesting in your behavior. In an attempt to achieve emotional survival, many of our protective mechanisms attempt to save the day, but often fall short at doing so. As I see it, it's not the moment alone that poses the biggest problem, but the feelings that accompany the experience and abound as a result of it. Though none of us have control over the fact that bad things can and do happen, we do have power over how long we allow these moments to affect our present and future circumstances.

As women, our personal power is not just effective toward others, it works for us, too. As a force of habit, we tend to view the concept of time as an ultimate healer. Although time is said to heal wounds, the assumption that it is the only needed remedy is false. It may help to diminish the visibility of your scars, but it will not serve to totally cure the injury. In addition to time, the quest for dominion requires action by way of acknowledgment, forgiveness, and sometimes disclosure.

Acknowledgment is often the hardest step because it totally confronts our mechanisms of avoidance and requires you exhibit a high level of honesty with yourself and others. It will demand you accept the fact that consistent denial, avoidance, and defensiveness do not work toward taking ownership of the incident and its influence on your life. Through acknowledgment you must confront the situation or circumstance and dissect the feelings attributed to the event(s). As you allow yourself to recognize your pain, you can expect to experience discomfort, vulnerability, and hesitation about emotions and wounds that may have never been truly realized or addressed before. Make no mistake, when you've been masking your pain for a long time, this can be a scary process. This first step toward dominion sets the stage for breaking through burdensome feelings and achieving a greater sense of control.

A MOMENT OF IMPACT MAY HAVE THE POWER TO AFFECT YOU, BUT IT DOES NOT HAVE THE POWER TO DEFINE YOU. WHY? GOD ALREADY COMPLETED AND PERFECTED THAT ASSIGNMENT.

As in the chapter about your God-view, a moment of impact may have the power to affect you, but it does not have the power to define you. Why? God already completed and perfected that assignment. Negative moments of impact may greatly challenge your personal journey but it does not have the authority to define, validate, or take away from God's view of you. Because none of us can afford to harbor a spirit that is wounded, your job is to meet your moments head on and effectively manage how they affect you.

In acknowledging the event, we must allow ourselves time to fully experience our emotions and take ownership of the moment/s as part of our personal story: "It happened and it happened to me." You have to embrace how you felt and how you feel. This step requires a great deal of support, so don't shy away from seeking professional help to get you through (e.g., therapy). Dealing with your feelings is necessary because you can't simultaneously live like you matter and remain stuck in a negative space that serves to distort and cloud who you really are.

Once you've fully engaged in the process of acknowledgement and acceptance, you will need to embark on the journey of forgiveness. First, you must be willing to forgive yourself for any unnecessary shame, guilt, or blame you may be carrying. In other words, take responsibility for the actions, decisions, and choices that belong to you, then be compassionate, understanding, and willing to stop relentlessly beating up on yourself. Remember, your spirit cannot thrive with you continuously kicking yourself.

Once you've addressed personal feelings toward yourself, those for others will also need your attention. Though circumstances and situations may differ, forgiving others is a vital part of the dominion process. Without fail, it is one of the best healers of the spirit and providers of a true sense of freedom. On the contrary, when we don't forgive, we create a cyclical sense of personal terrorism by fueling the negativity of the person and incident while giving them power over our disposition, decisions, and emotions. No matter how it may seem, forgiveness is not a stamp of approval or release of responsibility. This couldn't be further from the truth. In fact, forgiveness deemphasizes the power of those who hurt you while motivating your spirit to be empowered, try again, and control the only thing you can—yourself.

Forgiveness requires that you let go. It also forces you to assess how you truly feel about being pain free. Why? Over time, negative feelings may seem like permanent aspects of who we are, so getting rid of them may appear to be a loss in and of itself. Asking that we love ourselves enough to release anything that threatens our ability to love and feel loved, forgiveness holds love as the standard despite wrongdoing. It takes our moments of despair and offers the option of making those moments short lived. It is the foundation on which both dominion and resolution stand firm. In its essence, it promotes a future free and unrepresentative of the past. With it, a foundation for personal resolution is promoted and the possibilities for positive human interaction are endless. Without it, the human spirit struggles for peace and experiences varying levels of self-destruction.

SECRECY IS THE ENEMY'S PLAYGROUND.

Last but not least, within the quest for dominion, is the issue of disclosure (breaking the silence). In our attempt to hide, avoid, and deny moments that caused pain, anger, and shame, we can submerge ourselves in bubbles of secrecy that often serve to create and perpetuate further cycles of negativity and personal captivity. In many scenarios, disclosure is a necessary step toward closure and authority. No, disclosure is not always necessary, but this assessment should not be attached to fear of people's responses and reactions. Instead, it should be attached to the lack of relevance and significance perceived by you. Despite the discomfort it may cause others, you own the right to tell your stories. You have the right to talk through your experiences. There is too much on the line to make such a detrimental decision based on fear or the opinion of others.

In cases of sexual molestation, secrecy is almost a guarantee that someone else will be victimized. Secrecy is often a necessary incubator for negativity. This was no different for Gail. Like many others, disclosure was not an option she felt she could consider. She moved through an adulthood that was not only plagued with a disabling secret, but one compounded by insecurity, low self-esteem, and obesity. At the age of thirty, we spoke of her devastation with being sexually molested by her uncle. Holding onto the fear of being outcast or upsetting her family dynamic, she was unwilling to disclose her childhood trauma to her parents and siblings. As a result, she endured her own sense of emotional turmoil and captivity. Unable to confirm whether or not her siblings had endured the same circumstance, her silence could have been a potential backdrop for further offense. Still consumed by fear, guilt, and shame, she has yet to take authority and ownership of her story. However, even in situations like Gail's, hope remains in the fact that the choice to take dominion is afforded with every day of life. With that, her opportunity for change and restoration is still hers for the taking.

Though the quest for dominion is hard for all of us, each of us have what it takes to achieve it. You deserve to be free of the fear and prolonged hurt that moments of impact often impart, and you can free yourself. Every time I tell my story, authority over my moment is further solidified. Through encouraging survivors, my dominion offers hope, optimism, and insight to others. It is now my charge and yours to help other women understand that no moment is worth conquering their laughter, joy, and future happiness. As crucial as a moment of impact may be, living like we matter mandates that we take dominion. Not only do you owe it to yourself, you owe it to those who will use your experience to move beyond their own circumstances. No matter what, the benefit of dominion is worth it, and so are you!

Seven Critical Reminders for Your Journey Forward

- No matter your moment of impact, it does not have the power to define you.

- Dare to deal with your feelings so you can take authority over the event and the challenges it poses to your sense of wholeness.

- None of us can afford to harbor a spirit that is wounded. It's time to forgive, let go, and grow.

- You have the power to choose how long negative moments of impact affect you and your future circumstance. You have the power to render it powerless over your emotions, behaviors, and decisions.

- Engaging the help of a third party (e.g., a therapist) to support your journey to wholeness is a wise—not a weak—choice.

- You deserve to be free of the prolonged hurt that negative moments of impact inflict. No matter your circumstance, no moment of hurt is worth living without laughter, joy, and future happiness.

- You have the power to free you so don't settle for less than the dominion you deserve.

INSIGHT CORNER

1. Define at least two significant moments of impact that represent painful experiences in your life.

_____

_____

_____

_____

2. Do you feel like you have dominion over these experiences? If so, are there any other moments of impact that need to be considered?

_____

_____

_____

_____

a. For the moments of impact that are still in need of dominion, how did these experiences make you feel?

_____

_____

_____

_____

b. Why were these experiences painful for you? What did you do to put an immediate bandage on the wounds that resulted from these moments?

_____

_____

_____

c. How have you been dealing with your pain (e.g., overworking, overeating, avoidance, addiction, relationship sabotage, etc.)? How have moments affected or challenged your sense of wholeness?

_____

_____

_____

_____

3. What do you perceive forgiveness would mean in each of these situations?

_____

_____

_____

_____

a. If you are or have beaten up on yourself for a moment of impact, how could you start to move toward self-forgiveness?

_____

_____

_____

_____

b. As it relates to others, how can you move toward forgiving those involved in your defined moments of impact? What steps will you take to move toward forgiveness?

_____

_____

_____

_____

4. If you have tried to forgive and your moment(s) of impact continue(s) to have lingering effects on your life, what will you do to reach out and seek professional help?

_____

_____

_____

_____

a. What is your timeline to start this process?

_____

_____

_____

_____

5. How can you seek to turn your pain into power and use your journey to help someone else?

_____

_____

_____

_____

EMBRACE THE POTENTIAL OF RESOLUTION

Chapter 5:

NOT LIKE MY MOTHER

NOT OWNING AND REALIZING THE RIGHT
TO BE HAPPY DOES COME AT SOMEONE'S
EXPENSE: YOUR OWN.

BEING A WOMAN IS NO EASY TASK. The very nature of womanhood is complex and the achievement of happiness is one that still eludes too many of us. Maybe it's because happiness in its true essence is subjective. As a result, some of us still struggle with it because it's often regarded as an accidental circumstance rather than a deserved disposition, or better yet, we just don't feel that we know how to achieve it. Hence, many of us have been taught to believe that happiness is something to be yearned for but never truly realized.

As women, we have learned that true happiness is usually achieved at the expense of something or someone. Well, this premise is true. Not owning and realizing the right to be happy does come at someone's expense: your own. Instead, some of us have accepted that we may never experience contentment for long periods of time. We entertain options that celebrate a continuous cycle of going to sleep and waking up, wanting more for our lives, while being bogged down by our own personal baggage. Part of releasing this baggage comes from choosing ourselves through making an honest assessment of significant relationships and lessons learned from them.

This chapter and the next touch on two of the most influential people in most of our lives: our mothers (mother figures) and fathers (father figures). In doing so, it becomes clear how resolution within these relationships influence our achievement of wholeness.

I once heard my mother repeat a saying, "Children live what they learn." Though this statement should not be taken literally, it is fair to say that experiences from significant relationships create a symbolic road or pattern we tend to follow. Much of this road is created and paved through our childhood and adolescence. These years provide many bearers of knowledge. One of the master teachers during this time is clearly our mother or mother figure. Her influence on our womanhood is undeniable. Some of the finest lessons in choosing and not choosing to live like you matter came from what you learned within this relationship.

As I've listened to many women struggle with considering a concept that has the words "live" and "matter" in the same phrase, I can't help but think that the lessons learned in the mother-daughter dynamic have played a role in this challenge. In general, the mother-daughter dynamic is quite complex. In fact, it's probably one of the most complex relationships that girls experience because it symbolically represents a vertical relationship (one in which you—the daughter—look up to her—the mother—to help define your sense of self). Though this may take a minute or two to digest, it's true.

Your mother, like it or not, has often been used as the frame of reference from which you could freely compare your own growth and maturity. Her influence on your womanhood is undeniable.

Both consciously and subconsciously, she created a template that served to exemplify the "shoulds" and "shouldn'ts" of life. In every sense of the word, whether present or absent, she represented power in its most natural state: power by way of influence.

A significant part of our womanly essence is determined by the care she gave and the life she lived. When absent or dysfunctional, the yearning for or adoption of another is likened to the struggle a plant endures when it tries to survive with little or no care. Good, bad, or indifferent, your mother imparted value systems that were eventually held as rules to live by or stray from. Some of us hate to admit it, but we've all compared ourselves to our mother/mother figure. Rarely can we understand ourselves without considering her effect on our lives.

―――――――――― •◆• ――――――――――

SOME OF US WANT TO BE
JUST LIKE HER AND OTHERS WANT TO BE
NOTHING LIKE HER, BUT WHETHER WE
LOVE, DISLIKE, DON'T UNDERSTAND, OR
DON'T KNOW HER, THE COMPARISON TO
OUR MOTHER IS INEVITABLE.

―――――――――― •◆• ――――――――――

For most of us, our mother's guidance served as a footprint to move us toward womanhood. As many of us seek to live healthier lives, we have no choice but to question the source of our initial lessons in not choosing ourselves or living like we matter. As you think back, do you remember her having a sense of wholeness and personal fulfillment? If your definition of her happiness was characterized by her ability to be all things to all people or you felt like she always expected much for others but struggled to feel deserving of the same for herself, you are not alone. Though some of us had varying definitions, many of us still have mental snapshots of our mothers' experiences, struggles, and choices.

The positive ones were used as markers we wanted to experience in own personal journey. The negative ones prompted us to vow to never do certain things like her. The serious declaration "I will never do…like my mother" is one to pay close attention to. Women from all walks of life have made this statement on different occasions. While ignoring the implication of this statement, many of us have failed to recognize that the declaration itself is either connected to hurtful memories or a change in personal values. As a result, few of us have given intense thought to the items placed on the infamous never-to-do list.

I challenge you to ask yourself: What have I vowed to never do like my mother? This list may take a while for you to create. When you answer this question in the Insight Corner, you may find that you've created a list that's pretty long, but it won't get you struck down by lightning, I promise. Whether your mother/mother figure is a grand image you hold near and dear, or one you try to forget, serious thought toward this question tends to reveal significant baggage that often goes undetected. Why? Believe it or not, most of the items on this list probably highlight your mother's inability to love, choose, and/or regard herself. And, as you further dissect your list, you will find that as daughters, it's not enough to just say you "will never."

First, you must explore why you put each item on your list. Second, you must question why doing them would be such a wrong choice. Third, you must choose to acknowledge any similarities between your past and present choices and her experiences. Finally, you must make the necessary changes to stop repeating the same patterns you've vowed to abandon. As in the following example, your ability to identify the parallels in your quest for insight is critical.

When Monica noted she would "never dumb down and not assert herself" on her list, she had no idea the insight that was in store for her. She placed this item on her list when she thought about her mother remaining at a company for over ten years despite the limitations placed on her career ambitions. Though they had a good relationship, she viewed her mother as one who seldom disagreed or asserted her opinion. As a single career woman, Monica was definitely on the fast track. During her company tenure, she went through an informal executive development rotation, received great evaluations, and was no stranger to high profile opportunities. When her new boss arrived, she had great hopes for further career advancement. She embraced the team members that he brought with him and saw her professional experience as an asset.

After two years, much of what she knew had changed. For the first time in her career history, her evaluations were less than favorable. Though her productivity was still that of a high performing employee, the subjective aspects of her professionalism were questioned at every turn. She perceived being overlooked for promotions and felt that one of her colleagues, a believed crony of her boss, had taken credit for her work on numerous occasions. Before addressing the item on her never-to-do-list, Monica could not see any parallels between herself and her mother. However, once she started on the path, a couple of things came to her attention.

First and foremost, she had stopped liking her job eighteen months prior, but accepted in her mind that her boss being moved, promoted, or fired would be the only answer to her career getting back on track. In essence, she didn't embrace her own power to assert a change in her situation, and she wouldn't consider the option of leaving to find a more suitable fit. Instead, she placed the power of change on everyone else. Secondly, though she saw no basis for her negative evaluations, she didn't contest nor assert herself when given the feedback. She even chose not to approach her colleague about taking credit for her work.

Though it had not occurred to her before, she—like her mother—had an underlining fear and discomfort with confrontation. Through this exercise she was able to make the connection between her mother's life and the choices she was presently making in her own life. Monica recognized that her assertiveness and ambitions soared when things were good, but often took a detour when met with potential obstacles and confrontation. To break this pattern, she chose to start using honesty and integrity as a foundation from which to battle her fear of confrontation. She committed to communicating her points of view when placed in contentious situations despite her discomfort.

The first step in turning her situation around was realizing how stifling her thoughts essentially replicated what she accused her mother of doing. In not asserting herself, she suggested that her ideas and opinions did not deserve to be heard. She found this disrespect to be much more damaging than finding the courage to address the issues.

Continuing forward, she chose to meet with her boss and shared some of her challenges concerning her previous job evaluation. She was clear going in that the conversation was less about him changing her review and more about her being heard and placed on record for disagreeing with its content.

One step at a time she found the courage to use her voice and soon after hired a recruiter that successfully found her another place of employment. In holding herself accountable for moving beyond her fear, she was able to promote more authentic scenarios than what had been acceptable in her past.

Even with the most honorable intentions, mothers have often ignored that it's very difficult for a daughter to "do as I say and not as I do." I still call my mother and discuss past incidents that leave her surprised at how carefully I audited her every move. For me, she was the blueprint from which I polished my personal masterpiece—me. Like many of you, I learned a great deal from my mother. However, I also struggled to avoid some of her pitfalls. As I created my personal never-to-do list, I found an overarching theme: my mother was a consummate self-sacrificer. As you review your list, you may see a dominant theme or themes that come into play. Take note of them and embrace what they reveal to you. In my case, my mother's self-sacrifice was pretty dominant. This role was quite challenging for me because I viewed much of it as working to her detriment.

As I looked at my list, I saw various points that brought on feelings of betrayal for evaluating her despite the fact that she is such a wonderful woman. However, I had to keep digging beneath the surface to figure out some critical things for myself. Being open (as I am challenging you to be), I offer a personal example that will help you explore the things that you've placed on your own list in a more productive manner.

One revelation on my never-to-do list was a vow "to never have a marriage like my parents." Back then, if you asked what was wrong with their marriage, I would have offered the following statement: my father was a terrible husband. At first glance, you notice that this assessment conveniently excluded my mother. Now please believe me when I tell you life was never quite the same when I embraced the idea that she, too, should be part of that statement. As I sought to evaluate my opinion, I had to ask: Could my father have been a good husband for someone else and just not a good match for my mother? Answering this question meant one of two things: my mother either chose the wrong man or chose what she thought was the right man and decided to stay even when she figured out she was wrong.

Either answer resulted in my mother electing to stay in a broken covenant for more than thirty-five years before removing herself and being liberated. The realization that my mother played a role in perpetuating her own unhappiness was initially overwhelming. All too often, her actions demonstrated that her needs were nonexistent. She appeared to love her child, husband, home, friends, relatives, and job much more than she loved herself. In itself, this realization was painful to admit.

Further probing revealed similarities between her personal decisions and my own. This item, in particular, red flagged my own tolerance for negative behaviors in relationships. I discovered what I had previously justified as the behavior of a "good girlfriend" was really the continuation of a cycle. My mother didn't give herself permission to regard herself in her romantic relationship, and I was traveling down the same path. I, too, stayed in situations that were spiritually and emotionally destructive. In fact, dysfunction had become a familiar expectation. Until looking at this connection, I couldn't see that my choices in men were often based on my insecurities. Though I desired love and respect, I didn't feel worthy of it.

I was entering unfamiliar territory. In a strange way, I had developed an affinity for dysfunctional situations. I didn't feel much love for myself, so walking away rarely seemed like a viable option. Like my mother, I might leave or push the other person away temporarily but I would always return with a good justification for why the relationship could work.

As a proud daughter, I would describe my mother as an independent, intelligent, and accomplished woman. But I often wondered why she remained in a situation that represented emotional sabotage. As I pondered her motives, I realized my mother didn't see commitment and respect in a romantic relationship as being directly connected to her worth. Though a wise woman, she considered them deserving characteristics for others, but never quite enforced the expectation for herself. Despite being worn down by the marriage, she chose to stay. In looking at this, it occurred to me that my mother had never learned to receive; she only valued herself through giving.

I FIGURED OUT MY FIRST MISTAKE WAS THINKING THAT A PERSONAL DECLARATION TO NEVER BE LIKE MY MOTHER WAS ENOUGH TO KEEP ME FROM DOING IT.

I had two choices at this point: turn back or keep going and make some real progress. I chose the latter. I figured out that my first mistake was thinking that a personal declaration to never be like my mother was enough to keep me from doing it. For years I dated without connecting these dots. I was able to maintain my blissful ignorance by fabricating major differences between my relationships and the one my parents had.

For example, my father was emotionally unavailable, yet when I saw this quality in the men I dated, I would give it another name to avoid the fact that they were exhibiting the same qualities. Quite frankly, it was hard to swallow that I was setting the stage to do the same thing my mother had done. Once on this path, it was clear where I could end up if I didn't take a hard look at myself and dare to see the truth. Yes, I learned a great deal from her example, but did that really mean I was doomed to repeat it? Instead of settling, I had to move. I had to let my mother off the hook and put myself on it. Only then would I be in a position to make better choices.

Here was my first critical question: Besides imitating what I saw, what exactly did I get out of my dysfunctional relationships? The answer hit me like a ton of bricks: I perceived leaving my relationships as failure. Remaining in unhealthy relationships was not just acceptable because of familiarity; staying was appealing because it reduced my fear of failure. Somehow, I attached my entire sense of worth to whether or not my relationships were sustained. In most scenarios, I was one unhealthy part of an unhealthy situation.

I mean, what would I have done with someone who effectively communicated his feelings, was accountable for his actions, and had the necessary tools to promote our mutual contentment? I was never attracted to or felt good enough for men like that. So I picked relationships in which I could feel a false sense of triumph because I needed something to fix. Fixing the situation was my drug of choice. It made me feel valuable, powerful, and in control. The emotional cost of engaging in these relationships never occurred to me. My fear of inadequacy and failure guided my decisions and caused me to continue dating people who I should have never considered for long-term romances to begin with.

If I could learn to love myself first, functional men would see the love within me and conduct themselves in loving and positive ways that mirrored the way I treated myself. But it had to start with me. This item on my never-to-do list made that very clear.

As you will find when you go through your list, gaining insight is just that, a look inside you. You become keenly aware of your own reality. As you may discover in your own journey, I came across information that revealed I needed to save myself from my own hand of destruction.

First and foremost, I made the commitment to stop dating for a while. I also made a firm decision not to revisit old relationships that were previously revolving doors of comfort. I took the time to examine what made me feel devalued and powerless in the first place. I sought to make myself the new gauge of my own personal value.

After staying out of the dating game for over a year, I was ready to seek companionship rather than a need for validation. I changed my dating criteria. I was open to men who would respect my right to choose myself. I listened to my intuition and nipped in the bud unhealthy situations that were not good for me the moment they revealed themselves. As a result, I engaged for the first time in healthy dating relationships with appropriate, communicative, and men that had potential for a positive long-term connection. One of those men is now my husband and life partner.

I EMBRACED MY MOTHER'S PAST AS A WAY TO CHANGE THE CHOICES I WAS MAKING FOR MYSELF.

As I journeyed through the other four items on the rest of my never-to-do list the insight I gained was life changing. I was able to compare my mother and myself in the same mirror. I embraced her past as a way to change the choices I was making for myself. I admitted the truth: My mother did have an impact on what I expected, accepted, and rejected in my own womanhood. But she also gave me a choice, a chance to learn from her mistakes and overcome what she struggled with. Though a tall order, is it not the order given to every daughter?

Sara vowed to "never disregard her daughter's passion like her mother did." At a young age, Sara had a passion for hair, make-up, and fashion, however, her mother had clear designs on her having a nursing career. "Nursing was stable and respectable." Her mother was unwilling to help her cultivate her passion and was adamant against any attempts to do so. Growing up, her mother provided for their family's needs and was intent on having her way when she disapproved of any of her children's choices. When Sara's sister went off to nursing school, it was expected she would do the same and follow in her footsteps. When she rebelled and chose to become a hair and make-up artist, the walls almost came tumbling down. Her mother was totally against it, which caused a rift in their relationship for years. It wasn't until Sara became a stylist and businesswoman that their relationship got back on track.

Now a wife and mother, Sara saw the impact of her never-to-do item when she looked at her relationship with her own daughter. Slated to become a lawyer by all family members and childhood rec-ollection, Sara was very disappointed when her daughter shared she no longer held an authentic desire to become an attorney. Standing on the premise that her daughter was being irresponsible, indecisive, and immature, Sara was highly disappointed. She couldn't readily see the connection between what her mother had done to her and what she was doing to her daughter. Lacking insight, Sara fought the idea that there was a connection—her mother was trying to run her life whereas she was trying to save her daughter.

Throughout parenting, Sara had struggled to right all the wrongs from her relationship with her mother in her relationships with her kids. Convinced she had done so, she had a clear sense of resolve with everything on her list except this one. When she thought about why nursing was so important to her mother, she recognized financial independence was the one thing her mother struggled with most and the one thing she wanted most for her children. Battling her own financial and personal challenges, she became fixated on controlling the destination of her children. In doing so, she had strained her relationship with Sara.

The same way her mother used disapproval, judgment, and lack of support to try to navigate her destination, Sara was now doing the same thing to her daughter. Though she had her share of learning experiences, Sara was happy with what she was doing and felt her life would have been less than whole had she not followed her passion. Her daughter was now seeking permission to do the same. Sara could continue to do what she vowed to "never do" or she could chose to give to her daughter the support she once wanted. As a result, she chose to stay connected, be supportive, and keep the lines of communication open while allowing her daughter enough room to uncover her own passion and career path.

For most, this exercise promises to be exhausting, but the reality is we can either choose to embrace opportunities for insight or shy away from them. As you identify ways in which you have exhibited the same undesirable behaviors and decisions as your mother/mother figure, it's up to you to challenge yourself and figure out what you personally received from these experiences. When you decipher patterns that have been perpetuated in your own choices, you have to make the necessary changes. As you challenge yourself through this exercise, burdens will be lifted, clarity will shine through, and opportunities for resolution will be presented.

For many of you, your list will evidence items that will clearly reveal you have already taken the necessary steps to not imitate or repeat, however, if you see patterns that represent similar undesirable behaviors, dare to challenge yourself. Choose yourself by figuring out what you personally received from these experiences and what voids you were trying to fill. When you uncover the needs perpetuated in your own choices, you can move toward actions that promote necessary change.

In hindsight, I can admit this process felt horrible at first, but it ultimately served to help both me and my mother grow. I received a sense of freedom and boldness that words cannot describe. This part of the journey was so liberating, I decided to share it with the person needing to hear it the most, my mother. A year and a half later, with strength and courage (surpassed by few in my mind), she made the choice to change and moved toward a personal fight for her own life. For the first time in over thirty years, she embraced the right to choose herself and start living like she mattered!

For many mothers, their greatest wish is that their children enjoy a life that doesn't experience the same pain or repeat the same mistakes, but one that symbolizes fulfillment and happiness at its best. As you challenge yourself through this chapter's Insight Corner, it is my hope that you will move one step closer to making this wish come true.

Seven Critical Reminders for Your Journey Forward

- Pay close attention to the declaration "I will never do…like my mother" in choosing yourself. Do not fail to recognize that the declaration itself is either connected to hurtful memories or a shift in personal values.

- Your mother, like it or not, is a frame of reference by which you compare your own possibilities for growth. It's not enough to just say you "will never."

- When you go through your list, you'll find comparing your mother and yourself in the same mirror will help you embrace her past as a way to change the choices you may be making for yourself in the present.

- Explore why you put each item on your list, question why you've decided against doing them, and acknowledge any similarities between your choices and your mother's experiences.

- As you identify ways in which you have exhibited the same undesirable behaviors and decisions as your mother, be honest about what you personally received from these experiences and what voids you were trying to fill.

- Uncovering the needs perpetuated in your own choices will help you move toward action that promotes the necessary changes and help you stop repeating the same patterns you've vowed to abandon.

- As you challenge yourself, celebrate your courage to move forward and care for yourself.

INSIGHT CORNER

1. How would you describe the relationship between you and your
   mother/mother figure?

   _____

   _____

   _____

   _____

a. Do you see much of her (mannerisms, likes/dislikes, personality)
   in the person you are? If so, how? If not, why?

   _____

   _____

   _____

   _____

2. In the left column, list the things you wanted to do or have done like
   your mother/mother figure. In the right column name some things
   you have vowed to never do like your mother/mother figure.

THINGS TO EMULATE	THINGS TO NEVER DO
_____	_____
_____	_____
_____	_____
_____	_____
_____	_____

3. Examining each item, why would doing each thing listed in the right column be so terrible?

_____

_____

_____

_____

_____

4. Despite the items listed in the "Never-do" column, do you find yourself engaging in similar behaviors? If so, how do your behaviors or decisions seem similar?

_____

_____

_____

_____

5. How have the "Never-do" items affected your sense of emotional, spiritual, and physical fulfillment?

_____

_____

_____

_____

6. Thinking in terms of needs and fulfillment as they relate to the Never-do items that you have eliminated, what do you believe was the motive behind your behaviors?

_____

_____

_____

a. What did you receive as a result of your actions/decisions? What was in it for you?

_____

_____

_____

_____

b. What void(s) were you trying to fill as a result of your actions or decisions?

_____

_____

_____

_____

c. What fears were being sheltered or avoided as a result of your actions or decisions.

_____

_____

_____

_____

7. What will you do to stop the cycle from being perpetuated? Will you engage an accountability partner to help keep yourself accountable to this decision? If so, who?

_____

_____

_____

Chapter 6:

FROM DADDY'S GIRL TO DADDY BAGGAGE

FOR EVERY WOMAN, a positive father figure is truly worth its weight in gold. In society, the role of motherhood has received consistent attention. The importance of a father to the psychological prosperity of his children however, is rarely given the same merit. For men, the father/son relationship, like the mother/daughter dynamic is very similar. Intuitively, boys look to their father/father figure for guidance on how to become men. But what about the significance of fathers to their daughters? As girls, we experience an intricate bond with our fathers. We look to our mothers for an indication of who we will become and how we should conduct ourselves. Our fathers introduce how to interact with and be loved by the opposite sex. A father's presence, love, and communication is usually seen as one of our first forms of validation. As a result, many of our romantic experiences reflect attributes learned from this dynamic.

When positive, the father/daughter bond is one of the safest places to learn how to be treated. It teaches us how to accept ourselves, feel deserving of love, and give love. When strong, it is based on a foundation of respect, involvement, and trust. This foundation establishes a strong sense of security and esteem. Its impact is evidenced in many different aspects of our personal and professional lives.

If you have a positive father/daughter relationship, it is difficult to overlook its value in your life. A father's smiles, hugs, and confidence boosts work together to nurture a subconscious sense of worth. His example helps to validate that you deserve to be treated with respect and held in high regard. Men who provide this for their daughters deserve to be celebrated. Though no father is perfect, his positive presence sets the bar for what should be expected, accepted, and received by his daughter. These efforts often materialize in a high propensity for positive friendships, intimate relationships, and personal standards on the part of their daughters.

In my experience, I've found that women who have strong relationships with their fathers exhibit less insecurity, more optimism, and are more likely to choose themselves. By no means do these women have perfect lives, perfect encounters with romantic partners, or even claim a perfect childhood. Their positive father/daughter relationship, however, burdens them with less emotional baggage and prepares them to create and maintain healthier situations with others. For most of these women, the positive father/daughter connection was nurtured by three factors:

- Their father's commitment to being an active, responsive, and responsible parent.
- His positive treatment of their mother.
- His ability to give, receive, and exemplify love.

Consequently, emotional baggage often originates from deficiencies in one or more of these areas. The significance of these circumstances within our growth helps to explain why a negative father/daughter dynamic has the power to inflict gaping wounds to our self-esteem and sense of self worth. In fact, as the relationship grows in a dysfunctional direction, it fosters expertise in collecting and reinforcing negativity that bleeds into the rest of our lives.

Jeanine was raised by her mother. Her father was married and had a separate family but gave occasional financial assistance to help with her care. As a teenager she reached out to him once, but he was unavailable for anything beyond a conversation. The distance between them remained until she was an adult and sought his help to move forward in a challenging and costly career choice. Being financially independent and in a similar line of work, she thought this was the least he could do. With little resistance, her father gave the help she needed. As she grew more credible in her field, they engaged in more consistent communication, but their connection was superficial at best. Single, beautiful, and successful in her career, her failed relationships resembled a who's who list of noncommittal men.

Through her mother's encouragement, she was challenged to recognize that her relationship with her father was no more resolved than when she was a teenager questioning why he never came around. Watching her daughter experience one romantic misfortune after another, knowing she was still wounded, she challenged Jeanine to let go, forgive, and truly talk to her father. Jeanine's anger was based on unexplained choices, feelings of rejection, and the decision her father made to not be an active parent in her life. Not only had those feelings transcended her childhood, it was now a burden that unfairly influenced outcomes in personal relationships.

FOR MANY OF US, HEALING IN THIS RELATIONSHIP CAN BE A TORTUROUS BATTLE OF WILLS: THE WILL TO STAY ANGRY OR THE WILL TO BE FREE.

When a father is emotionally unavailable, struggling with a negative sense of his own manhood, or avoids his parent/teacher role, the consequences to his daughter are crucial. As little girls, we may yearn for but not recognize the void. However, the reality of how critical this relationship is to our esteem often lays dormant until a girl enters adolescence and early adulthood. Our insight to its effect often gains momentum when we start to relate to others intimately, define our roles with, and seek validation from the opposite sex. For this reason, negativity within the father/daughter relationship is a great predictor of problems to come.

For many of us, healing in this relationship can be a torturous battle of wills: the will to stay angry or the will to be free. Though it may be hard for us to accept, learning to choose ourselves requires healing the wounds of the father/daughter bond as an absolute necessity rather than luxury. In my personal journey, the road to resolved feelings for my father was tough and really stretched me.

THOUGH I FOUGHT TO STAY CONNECTED,
I RESENTED HIM FOR NOT BEING THE MAN
I ONCE THOUGHT HE WAS.

Like many of you, I was convinced I could just pick and choose what I wanted to resolve in my adulthood. The destructive power of unresolved relationships, however, was never more apparent than when I took a look at my relationship with my own father. The more I opened my eyes to the truth, the more I could see how not resolving my feelings for him was slowly destroying my own pursuit of happiness.

In my childhood, I had fond memories of my father. However, the closer I moved toward adolescence, the more my loving and respectful ideals of him seemed to fall apart. With maturity, I began to see how much he struggled with his role as a husband and a father. It was often difficult for him to provide stability for our family. More often than not, the consequences of his choices were painful, long-lasting, and unforgettable. As I witnessed the fighting, separations, and broken promises, my "daddy's girl" allegiance turned to disappointment and disrespect. Though I fought to stay connected, I resented him for not being the man I once thought he was. As time progressed, we talked less and argued more. While our relationship fell apart my mind asked, what was wrong with *him* as my heart wondered what was wrong with *me*. The more I identified my worth by his choices, the more devastated I became. With every battle, our relationship appeared to drift to the point of no return.

Like many women, I dealt with the intensity of my feelings through a mastery of illusion. I convinced myself that my issues with my father didn't affect me, matter, or mean anything. The reality behind this facade always surfaced when I attempted to make an intimate connection. Without fail, all my relational experiences served to intensify my unresolved feelings towards him. My emotional unavailability, combativeness, and fear of vulnerability were the telltale signs that something was seriously wrong.

Quite frankly, I wish I could say resolution was something I decided to embrace because I was a mature and good-hearted human being, but that would be dishonest. The truth is, my unresolved issues left me emotionally paralyzed. As it related to my father, I had decided the hurt he caused didn't deserve to be forgiven. As previously mentioned, many of us are beholden to the idea that forgiveness somehow endorses wrongdoing. Thus, it takes a long time to recognize that the price of resolving our feelings is far less than the price of continued avoidance. It takes even longer for us to embrace resolution as an act of choosing wholeness. Though risky and uncomfortable, resolution in this and every other relationship deserves as much energy as the negativity that often discourages us from it. As with the father/daughter bond, there are a myriad of circumstances that create valid justifications for our anger, indifference, and resentments. These circumstances often serve to encourage the notion that forgiveness is solely a gift to him rather than a gift to ourselves. This premise alone can make resolution seem impossible; however, we cannot ignore the outcome of intense negativity toward our fathers: the inability to give love, receive love, and be understood beyond the superficial.

For those of you who don't buy into the rationale that resolution within this relationship is important, I challenge you to give the premise more consideration. In recognizing none of us can reverse the hands of time, resolution stands to be the best any of us can hope to achieve. When we try to deny the need for resolution with our fathers, we rarely disguise what is internalized as a result of the hurt. Chances are, any person of significance in our intimate history can identify behaviors prompted by the negativity of or absence of this relationship. Though we continue to try, few of us have been successful at hiding the emotional seeds planted by this bond or the lack thereof. If you don't believe me, go to the first question in this chapter's Insight Corner and write down the names of your closest girlfriends. Put an X by the ones raised without their father's influence, two X's by those who were raised within a strained father/daughter dynamic, and put three X's by those who were raised by and seem to have strong and healthy relationships with their fathers. Now, look at the names that have three X's. What type of men do they attract? What type of romantic involvements do they have? What type of disposition do they have toward intimate relationships? I'll bet they act differently than the other women on your list. Part of this disparity pertains to what I call "daddy baggage." We all have a "daddy bag," but it's not the bag that presents the problem, it's the content.

It's like the difference between traveling with a suitcase full of coordinated outfits versus one full of clothes that don't match, need alterations, and don't complement your shoes. The content either promotes a sense of confidence and preparedness or one of anxiety and despair.

THEY ALL BELIEVED "DADDY BAGGAGE"
WAS A TRAFFIC ROADBLOCK THAT WARNED
THERE WAS DIFFICULTY UP AHEAD.

When I've discussed the "daddy baggage" concept with men, they not only agree that it exists, but the topic creates a good share of frustration as well. Though they can't speak for all men, they all declared "daddy baggage" was a traffic roadblock that warned there was difficulty up ahead. Some revealed the daddy baggage of women they dated often created an inability to foster a functional and peaceful relationship. Without knowing it, they suggested a woman's feelings toward her father were either revered, resolved, or suppressed. If, in fact, her feelings were suppressed and unresolved, the resulting residue usually reared its ugly head and undermined long-term relationship viability.

In conjunction with affecting success within relationships, the father/daughter dynamic also helps to create an "invisible billboard." This billboard suggests a figurative message/advertisement: verbal and nonverbal communication of personal boundaries (what you will and won't do) and baggage/brokenness (what you've experienced and not resolved) that either attracts people to or repels them from you. Whether positive or negative, the father/daughter relationship often influences the information we send out to those we encounter. For example, a woman who has witnessed continuous abuse at the hands of her father could be more apt to exemplify an ad of questionable self-worth, past experiences with violence, and patterns of dependence than one who hasn't. This ad would more than likely attract a mate who preys on the insecurities of others to create a false sense of power for himself. Our ability to confront denial, sadness, and unmet needs as they relate to our fathers gives us the best possible chance to change our message board and not relive similar circumstances.

I KNOW IT'S HARD TO ADMIT THAT SCARED AND HURT LITTLE GIRLS CAN GROW UP TO BE SCARED AND HURT WOMEN, BUT IT'S OFTEN A PREDICTABLE TRUTH.

For me, the resolution I experienced with my father was an exercise of my faith. It changed my demeanor and freed me to embrace my own potential for happiness. I know it's hard to admit that scared and hurt little girls can grow up to be scared and hurt women, but it's often a predictable truth. You may not be able to create a new relationship with your father, but you can refuse to further suffer from a wounded existence. This does not mean you should close your eyes to the man your father is, but it does mean you have to forgive, and at a minimum, put the relationship in perspective by letting go of unfulfilled expectations, broken promises, and perceived parental inadequacy.

Though a negative father/daughter relationship will never determine how much you deserve to be loved, it can debilitate your ability to embrace the notion of love. If you look beyond your anger, you will see that forgiveness is a priceless gift in loving yourself. When I let go of the negativity that had taken root in my heart, I was able to see my father. In doing so, I saw a man who experienced an intense amount of pain from a childhood plagued by rejection. I recognized his behavior was an extension of what he endured throughout his lifetime. I also accepted that his actions usually had little to do with his feelings for me, and more to do with his feelings for himself. On my own volition, I made the choice to accept him for who he is and refuse to continue being bitter.

Shortly after I resolved my issues with my father, we mutually agreed to work on reconciliation. We started over and decided to invest in moving forward in a more positive manner. I must specify however, there is a major difference between reconciliation, which is a collaborative effort (we), and resolution, which is a solo effort (I). When I sought to work through my father/daughter baggage, I did so without any permission, help, or cooperation from my dad. He was not a factor in my ability to successfully resolve my feelings for him. Our reconciliation was not a condition of my resolution because the ability to achieve resolution is not dependent on another person's behavior, it is an individual decision that depends on one person—you.

In conjunction with being empowered to resolve, we too, have the power to reach out to those we may have hurt and/or offended. Often, "I'm sorry" is just as much a blessing to us as it is to the person receiving it. Just as we want others to be accountable for how they treat us, it's our job to be accountable for how we affect the lives of others. And, the power of an apology is too frequently underestimated. As a sincere extension of remorse, whether accepted or not, it is often a first step in opening the path for positive dialogue.

When Debbie was seven years old, her mother died. Her father, unable to take on the responsibility, relinquished his role as a primary caregiver. For years, she struggled to find stability, security, and some semblance of normalcy. Though periodically living with relatives, she experienced a rather lonely childhood and fought to find her place in the world. As time passed, memories of her mother became harder to hold onto. What was once a traditional family had transformed to occasional visits with her father on weekends and holidays. It was clear that her mother had been the glue that held her family together.

As an adult, much of Debbie's sadness was based on losing her mother at such an early age. However, her once flourishing father/daughter relationship was also short-circuited by the turn of events, leaving her feeling even more abandoned. Though he was still alive, at times she felt as though both of her parents were gone. Upset and distant from her father for many years, she wouldn't own the need for resolution. When her own daughter was born, she changed her mind. Scared of being a new mother and of all the responsibility involved, for the first time she embraced her pain. She was angry that her father didn't take care of her when her mother passed away, she felt unloved, rejected, and not good enough for him to "fight" for.

As a new mother, she recognized how insecure he may have felt and how unprepared he may have been for what happened when her mom died. Unwilling to let the pain continue to fester and be potentially passed onto her child, she embraced the fullness of her emotions and moved to release the resentments she held onto for years. Resolved in her feelings toward her father, she approached him and offered an apology for holding such bitterness toward him for so many years. To her surprise, he reaffirmed his love for her, apologized for all that she had been through, and validated what she felt. From there, her resolution opened the door for reconciliation, a new beginning in their relationship, and a fresh start in his role as a grandparent.

Through all of these scenarios, it's fair to say resolution gave a lot more than what was taken by unforgiveness. The undying power of resolve is like a well of unending benefit. And, achieving it is symbolic of where you are on your way to loving and living like you matter.

Seven Critical Reminders for Your Journey Forward

- Learning to choose yourself requires healing any wounds that may exist from your relationship with your father.

- A lack of resolution in your father/daughter relationship is sure to cause negativity that bleeds into the rest of your life, so it's worth working through.

- The quest for resolution in this and every other relationship deserves as much energy as the negativity that will try to discourage you from it.

- Valid justifications for your anger, indifference, and/or inability to forgive do not negate the fact that intense negativity promotes being unable to give and receive love and establish a sense of personal wholeness.

- Letting go of unfulfilled expectations, broken promises, and parental inadequacy does not mean you have closed your eyes to the man your father is or was, but your quest for fulfillment depends on your ability to do so.

- Resolution is a solo effort, so you have the power to take the necessary steps toward achieving it.

- Resolution requires you to forgive. If you look beyond your anger, you will see that forgiveness is a priceless gift in loving yourself.

INSIGHT CORNER

1. Write down the names of your closest girlfriends.

_____

_____

_____

_____

_____

a) Put an X by the names of those raised without their father's influence.

b) Put two X's by those who were raised within a strained father/daughter relationship.

c) Put three X's by those who were raised by and seem to have strong and healthy relationships with their fathers.

d) Now, look at the names that have three X's. Think about the type of men they attract, the type of relationships they have, and the disposition they have toward relationships. Do you see a difference between them and the other friends listed?

2. What kind of man is/was your father/father figure?

_____

_____

_____

_____

3. Did you want him to be someone other than who he was? If so, what kind of man did you want him to be (e.g., kinder, more supportive, more active in his role as a father, etc.)?

_____

_____

_____

_____

4. What type of relationship do you presently have with your father/father figure?

_____

_____

_____

_____

a. If the relationship is positive, what can you do to acknowledge what his presence means to you?

_____

_____

_____

_____

b. If it is not positive, what type of feelings does it elicit? What is the basis for these feelings—what happened?

_____

_____

_____

c. What impact has this relationship had on you and your self-view (e.g., diminished confidence, self-worth, etc.)?

_____

_____

_____

_____

d. What would happen if you decided to acknowledge, purge, and let go of those negative feelings?

_____

_____

_____

_____

5. What will you do to move toward forgiving him and resolving your negative feelings (e.g., write a letter to him as an exercise in expressing your thoughts and releasing your feelings, contact him, etc.)?

_____

_____

_____

_____

STOP BEING INVISIBLE

Chapter 7:

RELATIONSHIPS:
TWO HALVES DON'T MAKE A
WHOLE

MANY PEOPLE SUGGEST THAT fulfillment requires the embrace of one's desires, dreams, and aspirations. Additionally, the realization of these elements involve some level of being prepared for moments that will bring them to fruition. Being ready when opportunity knocks is half the battle. Though preparation does not always guarantee success, the lack of it often works to its detriment. I believe this premise lends itself to many aspects of our lives, including the achievement of positive connections within love relationships. In an ironic sense, wholeness (physical, spiritual, and emotional health) and connection are related. As whole individuals, we are more likely to attract and experience functional romantic partnerships. Without denouncing the relevance of hard work, wholeness gives us the best chance at love.

Though married now, I've had my share of sour relationship experiences. As I struggled through one dating challenge after another, I began to think the connection I sought was unrealistic and unattainable. Either I gave too much or gave too little. Some relationships I sabotaged purposely, some I sabotaged unintentionally, and others I can admit were just flat-out bad choices. For a long time, I even believed something was wrong with all the men I dated.

If you feel this way, too, I want you to try something. Take your hand and make a fist, then use your index finger to point at something. Now, look at your hand as you point. Do you notice one finger aiming away from you and three pointing back at you? In other words, before we become quick to blame and label others, we may want to take an honest look at how prepared we are for a thriving connection.

In all of my past relationships, one element remained consistent—me. Once I acknowledged that fact, I could see none of them had a prayer of being much more than posters for dysfunction. Why? At the core of my being I was less than whole. I wasn't prepared to manifest the woman I wanted to be—much less prepared to engage in a healthy situation. I wasn't ready to love myself unconditionally, nurture my own heart daily, and choose balance consistently. As a result, I was unable to attract, receive, or succeed within the type of commitment I spent forever desiring. I wanted so much but was ready for so little.

In dissecting why many of my relationships were unfulfilling, I had to fully accept accountability for the disasters as well as the temporary successes. Though I look at each encounter as a learning experience, I wasted a lot of time and energy, with little to show for it. For the most part, I focused too much on others and too little on myself. I readily made personal alterations to please others, but rarely had the courage to just be myself.

Though I look at each encounter as a learning experience, I wasted a lot of time and energy, with little to show for it.

Thankfully, it didn't take me a lifetime to learn the mathematical notion of two halves making a whole doesn't work well in relationships. I was forced to see that my only true chance of getting the type of connection I wanted depended on my ability to first have a solid self-connection. Like many of my friends who were also having difficulties, I had yet to define myself.

When we think of the word "connection" in relationships, few would argue that it is a major goal. The human spirit thrives on connectedness in all kinds of relationships. However, we often choose the path of most resistance when seeking to achieve it on a romantic level. This is due in part to the fact that the more we connect with our own spirit, the more prepared we become to connect with the spirit of another. Far too many relationship disasters come from ignoring this premise.

Although my past romances had their good points, none of them were even close to what I thought I wanted. I use the word "thought" because the more I defined and understood myself, the more my desires evolved. The more I focused on my personal growth, the more I realized what I thought I wanted was a bit hazy to begin with. For the most part, what I wanted was nothing more than what I was told I should want and what I believed I could expect. It was a stretch to think my envisioned mate could complement me when I had yet to figure out what made me tick. Strangely enough, this revelation contains hope for all of us. I hope that if we focus on our own growth (e.g., diminishing our fears, celebrating our worth, moving within purpose, etc.), the romantic connection many of us desire might actually be attainable.

FEELING BOUND TO WHAT SHE THOUGHT SHE WANTED, SHE BECAME EMOTIONALLY DEPENDENT THOUGH HE WAS UNWILLING AND UNPREPARED TO COMMIT.

Mark was the catch most would say looked good in a frame—attractive, educated, and full of potential. Lisa dated him for more than three years, experiencing severe ups and downs. With infidelity and continuous commitment issues, she sought to find solace in promises yet fulfilled and the image of who Mark was. Feeling bound to what she thought she wanted, she became emotionally dependent though he was unwilling and unprepared to commit. Unable to break away, she accepted a six-month work assignment in another state. With minimal contact, she used the distance to recommit to her own sense of wholeness. In so doing, she gained perspective and discovered continuing in their pseudo-relationship would only serve to denounce the woman she was now ready to embrace. When she returned home, she moved forward and didn't turn back. Embracing her right to define and accept herself as is, she was ready for the real thing. When it came along in Travis, she was prepared to enter a mutual partnership.

As women, defining what we want for ourselves is critical. Many of us have minimized our boundaries, overlooked our personal rules, neglected sound advice, avoided obvious truths, and allowed our self-esteem to be destroyed, all in the mislabeled name of "love." Fortunately, love does not hold any of these requirements. True love gives ample room to promote care for ourselves. Like the heart, which symbolically pumps blood to itself first then the rest of the body, it, too, identifies the necessity of caring for itself so that it may adequately do its job.

Indeed, there are things companionship will provide, but the foundation of love for oneself won't be derived from being with someone else. In this same manner, we are required to care for and respect ourselves first so we may then do the same for others. This premise does not promote neglectful selflessness or selfishness. Instead, self-love employs honesty, integrity, and authenticity. It also affords an appreciation of what we see as our present self, requiring we love what we see in the mirror unconditionally. It promotes that you embrace who you are in addition to who you want to be. Herein lies the irony: Who you are (present emotional maturity, growth, and resolution) rather than who you want to be (future growth and maturity) often predicts who you attract. Why? As previously mentioned, some women may be masters of wearing a mask (which portrays them as being free of heavy emotional baggage), but they are only fooling themselves. In the romance department, much of what we try to suppress often shows itself in behaviors which indicate who we really are and end up attracting a mirror image of ourselves. For example, it seems befitting if you desire a mate who has a presence that commands respect, a good question to ask would be whether you conduct your life in a manner that promotes self-respect and respect from others. It makes sense, attracting the type of mate you want does relate to your ability to foster and nurture complimentary qualities within yourself.

Without taking anything away from the opposites-attract theory, similarities and complementary values play a significant role in forming the core of many successful relationships. Unlike a causal dating situation, beyond the physical attraction, a true connection is able to manifest as a result of work we've done prior to meeting the person. This type of work often determines our ability to promote long-term relationship viability. I found the closer I moved toward being the woman I wanted to be—the woman I was born to be— the more I chose to pass on relationships I would have previously set- tled for. Movement toward wholeness brought forth a level of hon- esty that made unproductive situations less tolerable. The more I embraced my own personal truths, the more I was able to perceive the true attributes of others. In essence, it prompted behaviors that kept my best interests at the forefront. This truth enables us to empower ourselves as a solo act, which increases our potential for success as part of a duo.

Once we're ready to receive a partner with whom we can have a connected relationship, maintaining wholeness while in the relationship presents a challenge all its own. Whether dating, com- mitted, engaged, or married, the expectations we put on ourselves, the ones we put on one another, and the ones expressed by society can pose threats to any romance.

How do we love someone else, maintain the needs of the union, and love ourselves at the same time? How do we fight off losing our sense of wholeness while in a relationship? The answer to both is we take it one day at a time and use teachable moments to our advantage every step of the way. Due to the fact that being in the right space when we enter a partnership does not eliminate the need to work at staying there for the duration, the use of teachable moments to engage our partners in the maintenance process is very, very necessary.

Whether or not we like to admit it, we teach people how to treat us. As we embrace the bliss of a loving connection, we often make the mistake of measuring our happiness solely by the happiness of our partner. I, like many others, have misused many teachable moments by choosing to be silent when I should have spoken up. From time to time, we've all made the mistake of being overly agreeable rather than forthright about our thoughts, feelings, likes and dislikes. While dating, I often chose to show how selfless I could be rather than how I needed to be treated. Instead, I gave all of my time and inadvertently taught my partners that I didn't need any time for myself. All too often we volunteer to change our minds and schedules, abandon positive friendships, and dismiss other healthy aspects of our lives, thus establishing a standard that dishonors living like we matter. As with many women, we have to keep reminding ourselves that our ability to maintain a strong connection does not require that we endlessly deprive and not attend to ourselves. Long-term maintenance requires we honor ourselves and give our mates an opportunity to do the same. Not only should we create opportunities to show them what is important to us, but when other opportunities arise, we should be prepared to take them.

IF WE DON'T CLEARLY COMMUNICATE OUR NEEDS, WE CREATE AN IMPRESSION THAT THEY ARE UNIMPORTANT. IF YOU ARE IN A RELATIONSHIP, IT'S UP TO YOU TO TEACH AND REINFORCE WHAT YOU WANT MAINTAINED FOR THE DURATION OF THE RELATIONSHIP.

In many circumstances, the use of effective communication and modeling of appropriate behaviors will help our partners learn what we want. In most connected partnerships, our mates do not intend to overlook our needs and desires. However, we often give them permission to do so. If we don't take the time to nurture ourselves, why would it even come up on our mate's radar that we are missing something critical to us? It is our responsibility to teach others to respect our needs with the same intensity we use to consider theirs. If our needs are not clearly communicated, we create an impression that they are unimportant. If you are in a relationship, it's up to you to teach and reinforce what you want maintained for the duration of the relationship. If you've been in a relationship for a long time, you have a bit more work to do because you have to help your partner unlearn what you've previously taught as the acceptable norm. In either case, now is not the time to feel helpless or overwhelmed. Now is the time to recognize that each day presents new opportunities to teach your mate new lessons regarding your needs and desires.

To maximize our teachable moments, we must start to relate to our mates in a manner that will best achieve our goals. Unfortunately, the communication barrier we've fallen prey to is based on communicating in ways we think are best versus ways the information will best be received by our mates. Think about it; if you speak English and the only language your mate understands is French, what good is it to communicate to him in English? Though you may have articulated your point clearly and concisely, he hasn't received a word you said because you delivered it in your language of choice not one that he understands. Repeating yourself in English, screaming in English, or being resentful in English won't get you satisfying results. However, if you speak your mate's language, you may uncover an opportunity to move out of the realm of misunderstandings and into the space where your needs can be acknowledged and your mate can take accountability for the results you desire.

I remember sharing an example with a group of women recently: John was tired and decided to take a nap. Joan, his wife, was tired too, but instead of resting, she chose to push through her exhaustion to check one more item off her "to-do" list. When John woke up, he felt refreshed and energized. He walked into the room where Joan was working and failed to pick up on the fact that she was irritable.

When John noticed something was wrong, the fact that Joan might be tired was nowhere on his list of reasons. Why? He figured tired people go to sleep; besides, he didn't tell her not to take a nap, so she must have recognized she really didn't need one. So, John looks to see if he took out the trash to make sure that wasn't it before he goes to ask: "What's wrong?" and she answers: "Nothing." Needless to say, I had a room full of laughing women on my hands, and we all confessed personal guilt in this area. In conclusion, we decided if the concept of wholeness could talk, it would probably say, "Joan, please, do us all a favor and just go to sleep."

On a very simple level, wholeness as it relates to relationships requires we move from some of our old comfort zones and create new ones which allow us to change and continue to grow. It requires that we have insight about what makes us feel safe, secure, and understood. In reality, having a connected relationship is not just about being chosen. It is also about being empowered enough as women to be sure the choice is mutual (your choice of a mate is just as important as your mate's choice of you). Once we see our value as whole individuals, not only will it promote success in finding the right one, but it stands to create a mutually accepting road your partner can take with you.

Seven Critical Reminders for Your Journey Forward

- Wholeness (physical, spiritual, and emotional health) and the ability to create a functional and thriving romantic partnership are directly connected.

- Getting the type of connection you want depends on your ability to first have a solid self-connection. The more you connect with your own spirit, the more prepared we become to connect with the spirit of another.

- As a rule of thumb, true love and connectedness give ample room to promote care for yourself. They do not require that you over-look your personal rules, neglect your inner voice, avoid obvious truths, or allow your self-esteem to be destroyed.

- Who you are (present emotional maturity, growth, and resolution) rather than who you want to be (future growth and maturity) often predicts who you attract.

- Similarities and complementary values play a significant role in forming the core of many successful relationships. Once the physical attraction is surpassed, the work we've done before meeting the person will determine your ability to promote long-term relationship viability.

- Maintaining wholeness once in a relationship, requires consistent attention. You must engage your partner in your quest to maintain a sense of wholeness (e.g., use of effective communication and modeling appropriate behaviors to help your partner learn what you want).

- If you love yourself enough to respect the qualities that promote growth and healing in your life, you can teach your mate to reciprocate in the same fashion.

INSIGHT CORNER

1. What does the concept of wholeness mean to you? Do you consider yourself to be a person who is experiencing a sense of physical, spiritual, and emotional balance? If not, why not?

_____

_____

_____

_____

2. What would a connected romantic relationship look like for you?

_____

_____

_____

_____

3. If you are presently in a relationship, does your mate respect your right to live like you matter?

_____

_____

_____

_____

4. Have you used teachable moments to communicate your needs to your partner? How can you best use them to help you maintain a sense of wholeness in your relationship?

_____

_____

_____

_____

5. What will you do to create a routine that chooses yourself and helps you maintain a personal sense of balance (e.g., make standing appointments to engage in a hobby, make time for spiritual devotionals, plan a weekend for friends once a quarter, exercising, etc.)?

_____

_____

_____

_____

Chapter 8:

IT'S NO LONGER FUN BEING A SUPERWOMAN

AS WOMEN, WE HAVE shaped our adulthood with the help of other women. For some of us, they inspired us to achieve greatness; for others, these women single-handedly motivated our personal ambitions and gave us the model of superwomanhood. They prided themselves on doing twenty hours of work in fifteen and passed on the same value system to us. In my case, their model taught me how to be a driven, multitasking machine. I remember looking back and wondering when I caught the "superwoman" bug. Though I can't pinpoint when it started, I remember moving toward the status of being a well-oiled machine living on fumes at the tender age of eighteen.

Unlike an automobile, I required little gas and minimal maintenance to keep going. Sleep, who needs sleep? Sleep was for babies, and I was seeking to conquer the world. Back then, youth made adult responsibilities and work-life balance seem light years away. Now older and wiser, I see things differently. It's no longer fun being a superwoman.

Now older and wiser, I see things differently. It's no longer fun being a superwoman.

Though you may have received many accolades for being the woman who can do it all, many of us have found that being a superwoman is no longer all it was once cracked up to be. As a recovered superwoman, I, too, remember the validation I received from others. So much so, it was almost worth staying that way—almost.

I was held in high regard by other women and felt a sense of acceptance and celebration even though I was killing myself by stretching myself way too thin most of the time. I became committed to not letting anyone know how I was feeling, not asking for help, not slowing down, and never settling for just doing three things at a time. Eating on the run, meeting deadlines, attending back-to-back meetings, reading emails, responding in record time, creating an action plan while listening to voicemail, returning phone calls, and reading reports—this was a morning in the life. Then I found out life wasn't just this way for me.

Blue-collar workers, entrepreneurs, and stay-at-home moms were not faring much better. With longer business days, frustrating commutes, greater family needs, and lengthier "to-do" lists, many of us were watching our days turn into never-ending, stress-filled moments. Striving to be successful, we entered a zone that often felt like a black hole. Even now, some of us still believe we can only get credit for being a good woman if we find ways to get results at all costs, require little rest, and act like we don't matter. But my question is: What are people really getting from us when we treat ourselves this way?

SUPERWOMANHOOD

DEMANDS THAT WE ASSESS OUR VALUE THROUGH THE EXTREMES OF BEING ALL THINGS TO ALL PEOPLE WITHOUT ANY NEED TO GIVE TO OURSELVES.

In chapter 7, I spoke about maintaining wholeness in romantic relationships. In this same vein, it is incumbent on us to see how wholeness begs that we abandon our allegiance to the superwoman lifestyle. Why? Often, living like a superwoman is counter to striving for balance. Superwomanhood demands that we assess our value through the extremes of being all things to all people without any need to give to ourselves. There are a few problems with trying to live up to such an expectation:

- No one person can do everything well, much less everything well at the same time.
- It's impossible to be all things to all people.
- All living things have needs—one being the need for rest.
- It's not possible to give our best to others when we give nothing to ourselves.

No matter how we intellectualize it, we were not meant to act like machines, and nothing from nothing leaves nothing, so we can't give what we don't have. However, I know bad habits are hard to break, so, as in my case, we may all need to enter a superwoman rehab of sorts. As I took various steps to wean myself off of what had become my way of life, I held fast to a couple of choices that promoted recovery from the superwoman bug. In doing so, I saw how they could prevent me from ever catching the bug again.

First and foremost, I chose to stop running myself ragged. While going nonstop, it never occurred to me that running myself down was negatively affecting everyone around me. Attempting to give more while running on empty cheats everyone from the fullness they deserve from us. As a full vessel, your cup will run over, and many will reap rewards from the overflow. Besides, most of the recipients of our exhausted efforts (e.g., our children, spouses, colleagues, etc.) would prefer if we refrained from what was causing us to be in such a bad mood and overextended state.

When Diane was given her promotion, she was prepared to be on the go for the first two months. A year later, nothing had slowed down. With a nearly insane schedule, she was constantly going. Though more frustrated, irritated, and unapproachable, she was convinced that everything was under control. Her view of the life that had now become an everyday hustle and bustle came into perspective on one unexpected evening. While preparing for the next day, her nine-year-old called for a family meeting. Hesitantly she agreed. When she did, her two daughters sat down with a newspaper and two old magazines and volunteered to help her find a job. When she reminded them she already had a job, they explained they wanted her to find a new one so she wouldn't have to be so tired and upset all the time. In Diane's case, her children saw the need to check her into superwoman rehab long before she did.

As I sought to take my recovery process seriously, it became apparent I had to stop breaking commitments to myself. Without fail, many of us are sincerely committed to doing what we promise to others, but rarely find the promises made to ourselves to be quite as important. It's not acceptable to let ourselves down regularly. If you said you would go for a fifteen minute walk to get your mind off work and get centered, why isn't that a necessary priority? Is everything else truly that much more important than you?

WE MUST SAVE OURSELVES FROM THE SELF-DESTRUCTIVE IDEA THAT ALL OF OUR TIME PLUS ALL OF OUR ENERGY EQUALS BEING A GOOD MOTHER, WIFE, MATE, AND WORKER.

Convinced she would never get back into shape after the birth of her second child, the idea of having enough time to exercise was unheard of for Lena. When committing to do so became one of her goals, she was a bit reluctant. When we went through her weekly schedule, she was surprised to see that a brisk half-hour walk was more about her not choosing to stick to the commitment she made to herself, and not about there being enough time. Throughout the process, she recognized how bad she had become at keeping her word to and valuing herself. Willing to try, she started by making a habit of keeping at least two of her self commitments. Now an avid walker with twenty pounds less weight to contend with, she learned the importance of using the same integrity she used with others when it came to doing things for herself.

Third, I recognized the words "guilt" and "good" don't work well for us when used in the same context. We must resist the urge to see guilty mother, wife, mate, and worker as another way of saying good mother, wife, mate, and worker. A good wife can decide to close the bathroom door for twenty minutes to take a bath without feeling guilty. Besides, isn't guilt for people who feel responsible for wrongdoing? So, why do we assign that label the moment we decide to do something for ourselves? Whether single, married, or parents, we must find appropriate ways to nurture ourselves. Healthy boundaries are not the enemy. We must save ourselves from the self-destructive idea that all of our time plus all of our energy equals being a good mother, wife, mate, and worker.

When Sonya continued to experience a struggle with achieving her goal of becoming an entrepreneur, it was clear she was in need of assistance. When I suggested she solicit the help of a responsible and capable college student to pick up her children from school and help them complete their homework two nights a week, she couldn't wrap her brain around the concept. This time would be critical and just what she needed; but the guilt of getting that type of help caused a moment of pause. Knowing she had to do something different to change her outcome, she chose to give it a try.

On the first night the young lady came over to assist Sonya's family, her eventual exit prompted the daughter to break into tears.

When Sonya asked what was wrong, she replied she wanted her new friend to stay. Needless to say her family was quick to adjust. And her decision did not affect her ability to maintain the "good mother" title. Through being committed to her own recovery process she was also able to care for their needs and her own.

I ALSO MADE A CONSCIOUS CHOICE TO STOP STRESSING MYSELF OUT! UNNECESSARY STRESS IS NOT A DESIGNER PURSE, SO IT'S TIME TO STOP TAKING IT EVERYWHERE WE GO.

Also, I made a conscious choice to stop stressing myself out! Unnecessary stress is not a designer purse, so it's time to stop taking it everywhere we go. Think about it; stress is one of the main reasons being a superwoman is no fun. The repercussions often force our bodies to show how displeased they are with our treatment of them, and we can literally become ill. The mental energy we put into stressing about whether things will work out could be better used having faith that they will. Doing our best and leaving destructive criticism behind is critical. Being our best to our friends, family, partners, and children doesn't require being continuously stressed. If we take it easy on ourselves, they'll more easily accept what we have to give.

For the same reason, we should stop believing we are the only people capable of doing all that needs to be done.

For the same reason, we should stop convincing ourselves we are the only people capable of doing all that needs to be done. Needing to do everything and doing everything within our set time—and done our way—is a major culprit of stress. Refusing to delegate and not being willing to ask for assistance is hazardous. It's not okay when more than half of your "to-do" list is made of items you've convinced yourself can't be done by anyone else.

For example, when I first got married, my husband went grocery shopping and came home with three boxes of the same cereal, among other oddities, because they were on sale. My first thought was, "I would have been better off doing it myself." That's the belief that usually gets us in trouble. True, I wouldn't have done it that way, but when was the last time buying three boxes of the same cereal caused a world crisis? Reverting to my superwoman days, I could have taken the shopping duty and placed it back on my list, but, having completed recovery, I forced myself to let it go and supported him in continuing to shop and get better at it on his own terms.

There is not simply one way to do certain things. Even worse, trying to do everything leaves no one else any chance to contribute to our lives. For our mates and our children, it limits opportunities to learn, share responsibilities, and work together for a common cause.

When Karin had her daughter, she proudly wore the "Super Mommy" crown. Dressing her daughter every morning was one of her many daily duties. When she returned to work from maternity leave, she tried to keep up her do-everything role. One week while working a conference, her husband dressed their daughter and took her for a play date. When she met up with them, she was less than pleased with the attire he chose for her to wear. For Karin, this was yet another thing only she could handle.

When I confronted her about designing a system in which she was the only person adequately skilled to do everything, she recognized the only thing she would ensure by doing so would be her husband disengaging from their partnership. Thus, judging and eliminating opportunities for him to grow and learn would eventually serve to promote his feeling capable of nothing, which would not be in their best interest. This possibility caused her to pull back a bit and applaud his efforts to be more involved in the overwhelming job of being the active and invested parent her daughter deserved.

For my own good, I also had to abstain from using the words "yes" and "sure" as default answers to every request. As a litmus test, if you're not saying "no" at least once a week, you might want to seriously question your recovery process. Our value as women is not based on how many times we say those two words. It is appropriate to say, "I'm not sure if I'll be able to do that, so let me take a moment to think about it and get back to you." It's also perfectly healthy to just say "no." However, if some of the people in your life only choose to understand the word "yes," you have two options: educate them about the new you or decide it's time to travel light and release the dead weight of that person or that person's expectations.

Ella was the administrative assistant to a well-respected pastor in her hometown. As such, her schedule often looked like a completed crossword puzzle—every time slot was often accounted for. Plagued with the word "yes," she started to see the pattern of every moment being one that others thought was owed to them. Not being able to say "no" had created weeks filled with what everybody else wanted and little of what she desired. When she committed to the rule of no unwanted activity for a twenty-four hour period once a week, she received her share of push back from those who felt she was unavailable to meet their needs. After two months of sticking to the rule, the flood of requests began to dissipate. In adding the word "no" to her vocabulary, she could actually see her goal of balance getting closer instead of being an impossible, out-of-reach ideal.

Another critical step in my recovery process was my decision to start taking time for the three R's (Reflection, Relaxation, and Rejuvenation) and the three F's (Faith, Fun, and Fellowship). When I stopped regarding them as inconvenient, unrealistic, and/or unnecessary time-consuming things that took me away from my "to-do" lists, I had an opportunity to see their true benefit. In our quest for wholeness, these items are a must. Thinking outside the box to uncover and call upon your resources to find opportunities for renewal is critical. There is nothing weak about soliciting help and pulling in resources to give you a reprieve. You may be surprised by how pleased others may be that you're reaching out for assistance.

Driven and dedicated to her profession, Felicia found great fulfillment in helping people transition to new careers. Without a doubt, she was doing what she loved and continued to be proud of being the wife and mother of a healthy family. In the past, working in a job she loved and caring for her family were seen to be the only forms of relaxation she needed.

When I assigned her to take a trip to a Zen garden with a journal in hand, she was unconvinced of its necessity or potential benefit. She was required to go alone, stay for at least three hours, and prohibited from the cell phone or anything that resembled work. Using this guideline, she explored the garden, treated herself to lunch, and wrote about what she had to be grateful for that week. When we next spoke, I visited the concept of the three R's (Reflection, Relaxation, and Rejuvenation) with her. Surprised at how well it related to her, she was urged to change her previous assumption. She quickly understood how much renewing her spirit helped her focus and refuel her energy for both home and work.

Like Felicia, Kris was able to see the utility of the three F's (Faith, Fun, and Fellowship) in somewhat the same manner. A self-proclaimed perfectionist, she lived a rather regimented life. For the most part, things had to be results-driven to be considered necessary. When she discussed her husband's complaint that she was way too serious and not enjoying life, she was challenged to step out of her comfort zone. Hesitant to do so, she agreed to join a women's group at her church and make a monthly dinner date with two of her girlfriends.

To her surprise, she could see how fellowship with other powerful women might potentially pour into her life. Both commitments helped her see how spending time to cultivate new and old relationships might be beneficial. With every week holding 168 hours in it, both Felicia and Kris recognized how devoting two to three little hours to themselves made a big and significant difference in how they felt and ultimately connected with their loved ones.

Together, all of these tools should be used to achieve a needed state of balance. We don't need a title to be a super woman. Without being a workaholic, wifeaholic, friendaholic, or momaholic, we are still valuable contributors to the lives of those around us. Now, let me caution you, not everyone around you will be happy about your progress. After all, some people may have something to lose from your being healthy and doing less for them. When we stay unhealthy, they don't have to be accountable for their actions, and they know what they can demand from us. So as you spend your time more wisely, you may experience resistance from a colleague, spouse, family member, friend—even your children. Despite the opposition from others, you must overcome the urge to relapse and revert to your old ways.

Now is the time to start grabbing back a few minutes in your day-to-day routine. For those of you who still need help creating new habits, I suggest you try taking the pinch test. In your day planner, place the words "pinch test" on one day of every week. On that specified day, pinch yourself to make sure you're still alive. Then ask yourself, what have I done to actively engage in my superwoman recovery process this week? If the answer is nothing, pinch yourself a little harder and carve out some free time. When you do, you'll embark on experiencing what every real super woman deserves: a sense of peace, empowerment, and centeredness.

Seven Critical Reminders for Your Journey Forward

- Superwomanhood demands you assess your value through the extremes of being all things to all people without any need to give to yourself. Living this way is counter to that of striving for wholeness.

- It's time to stop running yourself ragged, stressing yourself out, and breaking commitments to yourself. Your recovery process mandates it.

- All of your time plus all of your energy does not equal being a good mother, wife, mate, and worker. It is a self-destructive equation that is not in the best interest of your health and that of those you care about.

- Delegation and collaboration are your friends, not your enemies. It's time to stop believing you are the only person capable of doing all that needs to be done and solicit some help.

- "No" is not a bad word, so dare to stop using the words "Yes" and "Sure" as default answers to every request.

- Taking time for the three R's (Reflection, Relaxation, and Rejuvenation) and the three F's (Faith, Fun, and Fellowship) needs to be as habitual and intentional as taking time for your personal hygiene. It, too, needs to be an everyday commitment.

• As you take your recovery seriously, start taking back a few minutes in your day and be ready to feel blessed and be a blessing to others.

Insight Corner

1. What superwoman symptoms do you presently exhibit?

_____

_____

_____

_____

2. What choices can you make to engage in a superwoman recovery
   process of your own?

_____

_____

_____

_____

a. If you have children, how might you give them an opportunity to
   honor and respect those choices? What will you do to start helping them understand that your recovery is not a rejection but a
   celebration of all that you want to give to your relationship with
   them?

_____

_____

_____

_____

3. Knowing that change is not liked by everyone, what will you do to deal with the resistance and discomfort on the part of friends, colleagues, family, etc., as it relates to leaving your superwoman days behind?

_____

_____

_____

_____

4. What can you do this week to release duties that represent you taking on more than you should? Who will you tell of your recovery plan to help keep yourself accountable to these decisions?

_____

_____

_____

_____

MOVE IN THE DIVINE DIRECTION

Chapter 9:

LISTEN TO YOUR HEART, HEAR YOUR PURPOSE

WHAT AM I HERE FOR? What is my calling? What was I meant to do with my life? Questions, questions, and more questions, all related to one word: purpose. That powerful word has varying effects on all of us. If you don't believe me, the next time you meet with a group of friends, ask them what they believe their personal purpose is. Once the question is posed, be ready to witness looks of intense thought followed by a myriad of philosophical statements, jumbled sentences, and extensive conversation all proving that you have just sent their minds into complete overdrive.

This question can either create a sense of despair, anxiety, and confusion or happiness, excitement, and peace. Why? Because the question usually triggers related thoughts like: Where am I going with my life? Am I truly happy? Should I be doing something else? Am I doing what I was put on this earth to do?

The complexity of these questions forces us to feel discomfort with the mundane aspects of life. They make it hard to ignore our passions, talents, and sources of inspiration. It forces us to look beyond the conventions with which many of us were brought up, like going to school to get a job that financially supports you. It promotes a stretch toward what I call the heart-driven approach—identify what inspires you, what you're gifted in, passionate about, and then pursue it.

Though many of us have felt obligated or fallen prey to the conventional approach, the latter is more applicable to finding and living within the true potential of one's purpose. By its very nature, living with purpose is the sweet spot from which satisfaction, humanitarianism, joy, blessings, and prosperity flow at their fullest.

In general, conversations about purpose are very thought-provoking. We have four options when pressed about questions of purpose:

1. We choose to evade the question and justify what we're doing at present.

2. We contemplate the question and get stuck because we don't know how to move forward.

3. We become saddened because we haven't moved toward our known purpose, and therefore feel immobilized from ever moving forward.

4. We contemplate the question, and with or without knowing how, we decide to embark on a journey of discovering that purpose.

From a personal perspective, I have contemplated the question of purpose too many times to count. I finally decided to stop avoiding it and made the scary decision to try and find the answer. Like many women, I realized very early in adulthood that life could be okay if I just decided to do the basics: get a job and acquire a few material possessions. No one would be disappointed in me—no one except me. Many people have settled for less because they have convinced themselves that a personal purpose in life is nonexistent, too hard to attain, or too late to achieve.

MANY PEOPLE HAVE SETTLED FOR LESS BECAUSE THEY HAVE CONVINCED THEMSELVES THAT A PERSONAL PURPOSE IN LIFE IS NONEXISTENT, TOO HARD TO ATTAIN, OR TOO LATE TO ACHIEVE.

Some have swallowed the myth that purpose is a once-in-a-lifetime opportunity that they missed. Others have become experts at explaining why they can't embrace purpose rather than why they can. However, we shouldn't see fulfilling our purpose as a luxury. Think about it: If we are all here for a God-given reason, the world is waiting to receive what each of us was brought here to offer. If part of your purpose is to be a writer, your future readers are waiting to be affected by the words you'll write. If you don't write, you prevent readers from receiving the benefit intended. Purpose is one of the greatest ways we could ever hope to give the best of ourselves to the world in which we live. We can fully engage in the art of giving through doing what God intended.

If you wonder whether you may have settled for less, assess how many times a month you feel like you're not doing what you love. What inspires you? What do you feel passionate about? If you don't have many fingers left, you might be misusing your energy.

It matters not your age or circumstance; what matters is how much you are willing to trust your heart and think outside of the box to embrace the personal journey.

For example, if you are a forty-two-year-old woman whose heart desires to work with the physically and mentally challenged, have you engaged in a process that will move you toward living in your calling? If at the age of forty-two you are struggling with why this desire is not realistic at this point in your life, consider the fact that you probably heard whispers of this same yearning at ages twenty, twenty-three, twenty-eight, thirty, thirty-four, and thirty-eight. Despite the checked items on your wish list, such as a romantic partner, house, kids, or job promotion, this voice still won't shut up! Well, it's time to recognize that this void will not disappear. So look forward to hearing from it again at forty-five, fifty, and fifty-five unless you do something about it.

YOUR HEART WILL ALWAYS REMIND YOU
THAT YOU ARE NOT DOING WHAT YOU
SHOULD. THE MORE YOU TRY TO IGNORE
YOUR PURPOSE, THE MORE IT WILL REFUSE
TO BE IGNORED.

You can almost guarantee that your heart will always remind you that you are not doing what you should. The more you try to ignore your purpose, the more it will refuse to be ignored. Though

I experienced a temporary sense of security from my strong friendship with denial, I couldn't stand spending a lifetime of wishing and never seeking to pursue my heart's desire.

If I listened—devoid of fear or doubt—I would discover what inspired me could provide hints about what the world was waiting to receive from me. Most of us have at least a minimal sense of our sources of inspiration, passion, and talents. We are often socialized however, to suppress these aspects of ourselves rather than explore them. As a result, many of us speak of these elements in the past tense: I wanted to, I wish I had, If I knew then, etc. If you are reading this book, it's definitely not too late to find and move within your purpose.

Despite what you have experienced in this life, purpose is a part of God's plan for each of us. The question is not whether or not we have a purpose. It's more about gaining clarity on what that purpose is. For example, Yvette challenged this premise by asking, "What if you don't have any gifts and nothing inspires you? What do you do if you are that person?"

I answered by saying, "That's not possible."

She then said, "What if you don't like to do anything in particular? What if the only thing you like to do is eat, what's the purpose in that?"

To her surprise I then said, "Eating is a legitimate passion. Food Critics, Chefs, Restaurateurs, Food Writers, and Nutritionists, the list goes on and on—their passion for food is a significant foundation for their craft."

In saying that, I recognized how many of us are thrown off our God-given path of purpose by our habit of discrediting the little things.

WE PRAY FOR PURPOSE TO BE REVEALED, AND WHEN SOMETHING REVEALS ITSELF, WE DISREGARD IT AS TRIVIAL.

We walk around minimizing utterances of the heart due to a lack of respect for the little things. We pray for purpose to be revealed, and when something reveals itself, we disregard it as trivial. As a coach, I treasure the power in the little things. When I help a client examine her life to find indicators of joy, inspiration, and intense feeling, the little things often mean a great deal. Little bits of insight, fond memories, and/or troubling circumstances often fit together to send a message from the heart.

Continuing down this path, I shared with Yvette, the example of how a young lady by the name of Denice found her way to purpose. Unclear at first of her purpose, when Denice spoke of how she loved to travel and had traveled all over the world, her excitement was contagious. However, all she ever remembered from her trips were the places she visited and the food she ate. Seizing upon this idea, she realized those two small things were indicators of purpose. As a result, she decided to go to culinary school and explore her passion for food. From there, she became a chef and opened her own restaurant. Though in the conventional sense, eating may not be regarded as something great, it happened to be her purpose-driven path. For her, this moment of insight flourished into its intended greatness once given the permission to materialize.

We each have a calling or two, for which our life was given. Being very visual, I see talent, passion, and points of inspiration as God-given seeds that were placed in our hearts to direct the identification of purpose. To accomplish the practical goals of life, we often move away from these indicators rather than cultivate them. As many of us recognized talents that had no conventional career path, some of us allowed our passion to turn into hobbies or we sought to suppress them entirely. In that process alone, many of us were told, "matters of the heart don't pay the rent." As a result, the acknowledgment of and achievement of purpose was not always seen as the most reward-ing and realistic goal for which to strive. Yet, this example does allow us to more readily see how the importance of using the heart-driven approach may have gotten distorted.

I know it may sound a bit simplified, but what does your heart say? Don't catalog your perceived failures or responsibilities, or consult your friends. We are so quick to negate how significant the heart is to defining purpose. We so rarely give permission for it to speak. The critical connection between the heart and purpose is one of the main reasons why a heart that's been broken by lack of resolu-tion, trauma, self-loathing, and the like, needs to be mended. Although a wounded heart speaks, often our ability to hear what it has to say is clouded by its bruises.

Thus, it makes sense that the best way to see the heart-approach in action is through talking to children. Interacting with them, you quickly realize children tend to dream out loud. They love what they love and they feel no need to apologize for it. They gravitate toward what connects to their heartstrings, and if they could, they would spend all day doing whatever that is.

As a little girl, Tina loved and had a special connection with insects and animals with which most people would probably feel some discomfort. She had a genuine fascination with animal books, animal shows on television, and pet stores. Tina talked with her mother about her fascination and realized her mother wished she were a bit less curious. Out of a concern for Tina's safety and the desire for her to gain an interest in other things she thought would be more suitable, her mom inadvertently tried to deter her passion. However, I spoke with her about a conversation I had with a wonderful veterinarian I know. She, too, had a similar childhood love for animals and her choice to become a veterinarian was based on that kind of passion. As a result, I talked Tina's mom and encouraged her to be one of the first to validate that Tina's love for animals was divinely placed even though she didn't quite share or understand it. I also encouraged her to help her cultivate her daughter's love (e.g., buy her a pet) and explore it (e.g., avail opportunities like visiting the zoo for her to learn and discern what she loved about animals) rather than feel the need to make her disconnect from it.

As we embrace our God-view, take authority of our past, and welcome the power of resolution, we give our hearts permission to turn up the volume on what it has to declare to us. And it's high time we listen. We need to pray for direction and open up to reading the clues within our laughter, wonder, and fascination to see what rises to the surface.

AS WE EMBRACE OUR GOD-VIEW, TAKE
AUTHORITY OF OUR PAST, AND WELCOME THE
POWER OF RESOLUTION, WE GIVE OUR HEART
PERMISSION TO TURN UP THE VOLUME ON
WHAT IT HAS TO DECLARE.

When I looked beyond my own self-doubt, I recognized there was so much to hear in my own heart. That's how my life's purpose was revealed. When I thought of what made me happiest, I had to take an honest inventory of my God-given gifts and talents and dare to stop doubting myself. When I listened, speckled throughout my fondest and most daunting memories was the recognition that I had a gift of song and seemed most fulfilled when I was helping to empower others. For me, empowering others through songs and words, both written and spoken, is the purpose within which I strive to live my every day. Like you, God gave me a heart that serves many functions. Finding my life purpose was one of them. So again, what does your heart have to say?

SEVEN CRITICAL REMINDERS FOR YOUR JOURNEY FORWARD

- The heart-driven approach to purpose is your divine direction for moving within God's design for your life. It is the sweet spot from which your satisfaction, humanitarianism, joy, blessings, and prosperity will flow at its fullest.

- Talent, passion, and points of inspiration were placed in your heart to direct the identification of your purpose. Look beyond the conventional script and stretch toward the heart-driven approach of what inspires you and pursue it.

- The question is not whether or not you have a purpose. It's more about gaining clarity on what it is. Take heed to the little bits of insight, fond memories, and/or troubling circumstances that may fit together to form messages your heart seeks to convey to you. Don't be thrown off your God-given path by discrediting the little things.

- As you embrace your God-view, take authority of your past and welcome the power of resolution; give your heart permission to turn up the volume on what it has to declare to you.

- The world is waiting to receive what you were brought here to offer. Purpose is one of the greatest ways you could ever hope to give the best of yourself to the rest of the world. If you don't live within your purpose, you prevent others from receiving the benefit you were intended to bestow.

• Listening to what inspires you can provide hints about what the world is waiting to receive from you. Don't move away from these elements; move within the cultivation and fullness of them.

• It matters not your age and circumstance; what matters is how much you are willing to trust your heart and think outside of the box to embrace your purpose-led journey.

INSIGHT CORNER

1. Do you feel you are presently moving within your heart-directed purpose? If not, why not?

_____

_____

_____

_____

2. What does your heart say about your personal purpose?

_____

_____

_____

_____

3. Have you prayed for direction as it relates to your purpose? What clues might be present in your life story when you think of moments that prompted laughter, joy, pain, and wonder? What rises to the surface when you think of those times or events?

_____

_____

_____

_____

a. What are you passionate about?

_____

_____

_____

b. What are your gifts and God-given talents?

_____

_____

_____

_____

c. What do you really enjoy doing?

_____

_____

_____

_____

d. What inspires you (both positive things and troubling things that you would like to see changed)?

_____

_____

_____

_____

4. Have you chosen to explore any of your passions, gifts, or talents as a career or a major portion of your livelihood? If not, what will you do to change that?

_____

_____

_____

_____

Chapter 10:

AND THEN THERE WAS VISION

THOUGH WE MAY HATE to admit it, most men would agree that women are the greatest consumers of products and services. More bluntly, men often accuse our entire gender of being never-ending shopaholics. We spend billions of dollars a year, but few of us consider the corporate vision of the businesses we patronize. Though vision may not be at the forefront of our minds as consumers, its significance is unparalleled. It is so important to the development of what we spend our money on, the success and profitability of a business often depends on it.

As women, vision is as critical to our personal purpose as it is to business. Now, how do purpose and vision fit? In Chapter nine we saw that purpose is often defined through listening to one's heart to discover what I consider to be "the three": God-given gifts, passion, and inspiration. For example, when I look at a painting, I think of how those three components manifest in the strokes of an artist's paintbrush. For the artist, the vision of what will be created is a culmination of passion, inspiration, and talent used to sort the array of colors and navigate the strokes of the paintbrush to create a piece of art.

For each of us, once we have discovered "the three", we must let our minds receive and develop the mental picture (or vision) that invites exploration. Vision helps to direct the journey; it's a projection of the destination (what is to come). Ultimately, the vision navigates what things are done, how things are done, when things are done, what resources are needed, what fits, and what doesn't fit. Vision is what most empires are built on. It's no different for us.

ATTITUDE AND EXPECTATION DICTATE THE PROBABILITY OF A VISION COMING TO FRUITION.

To this end, I believe that attitude and expectation dictate the probability of a vision coming to fruition. Those who first master-minded the vision of humans walking on the moon could have never realized that dream if they hadn't possessed the appropriate attitude and expectation that it could happen.

When I met Nora, her interests were intriguing to me. She was the only woman I knew who was passionate about flying. Years later, I learned more about her interests, and was fascinated by the commitment and planning she invested in her vision of becoming a pilot. With confidence and intent, she believed she was one of the chosen few to walk this path. She focused less on the odds against her and more on her attitude, efforts, and the expectation her vision would manifest itself in a mighty way. Though it was an extremely competitive and male-dominated specialty, she was determined to not be deterred or distracted.

Unlike some, she saw the power of declaring her vision on paper: to succeed at becoming a pilot and broadening the horizons of children to what God can do through them in this unconventional yet fascinating career. It was a reminder of where she was going and what she was working toward. In a subtle way, it solidified her agreement with God to pursue what had been given to her as the purpose for her life. The last time we spoke, she successfully checked a great deal of critical items off her action plan, one of which was the completion of her pilot training and the other was that of completing her journey to a foreign country to mentor and expose kids to her passion for flight.

WHEN WE BELIEVE IN OUR GOD-VIEW, WE CAN EMBRACE THAT GOD VALUES US AND THAT WE ARE DESERVING OF A GOD-GIVEN VISION FOR OUR LIVES.

Together, faith and self-appreciation fertilize the concept of vision. When we believe in our God-view, we can embrace that God values us and that we are deserving of a God-given vision for our lives. We can accept that there is a command post with our name on it. However, when you continuously question who you are, it's easy to think you would never be enough for God to pour a divine assignment into. But who better than you? Don't you think God evaluated the fit of your purpose before it was given to you? Companies go to great lengths to make sure potential employees are the right fit, as did God when matching your spirit in the assignment of purpose.

With boldness, it's up to us to embrace, see, and declare the vision with great expectations. Without a declared vision, dreams are floating fragments that are paralyzed by not being given permission to become a full picture. If some of the proud women who changed the course of history were unable to accept the power of their purpose, where would we be? Where you are doesn't matter as much as where you see yourself going. Vision is the difference.

When Maxine envisioned starting an entrepreneurial venture as being part of the manifestation of her purpose, she had no financing to bring her dream to fruition. With faith and expectation she made her vision clear by writing it down. Then when asked by a financial institution to share projections for where she saw her business going, she was more prepared to do so. She quickly realized if she couldn't own the vision and celebrate being the person to bring it to fruition, she wouldn't be able to convince anyone else to come on board. In this instance, her attitude and expectation had a great deal to do with how far she would "cast her net". She had to take courage in accepting the breadth of her assignment and believe that God could see her through any obstacle. She chose to not let fear dominate her process nor let feasibility cause her to retreat. After her share of rejections, she was adequately funded and her establishment was blessed to open just like God had promised.

Someone once told me that the woman who thinks she can and the woman who thinks she can't are both right. That rang true for me. What you expect will happen in conjunction with what you think you can or can't do is what makes or breaks you.

———————•➤•———————

GOD GAVE THE VISION TO YOU, SO YOU'RE
THE ONLY ONE WHO HAS TO EMBRACE IT IN
ITS INITIAL PHASES. DARE TO GIVE YOUR
HEART THE FREEDOM TO HAVE ITS SAY
WITHOUT THE COMMENTS OF OTHER
PEOPLE GETTING IN THE WAY.

———————•➤•———————

Transferring the desires from your heart to a piece of paper is as good a first step as any. Even if at first it seems too fragmented, out of the ordinary, or too big, it's a start toward a clearer picture and your commitment to move toward it.

You've probably noticed I said place it on a piece of paper. I didn't say, "be quick to tell a group of your friends." Why? You can never assume that people are whole enough to embrace your personal insight. Additionally, it's never guaranteed people will buy into your vision—and, that's a curve ball that takes us a while to recover from. The good thing is, they don't have to buy into your vision for it to be right on. God gave the vision to you, so you're the only one who has to embrace it in its initial phases. Dare to give your heart the freedom to have its say without the comments of other people getting in the way. Besides the people needed to *realize* the vision, you only need one or two people to encourage your movement and support your under-taking in the initial phases.

When Leana was given the opportunity to come to America, she didn't hesitate for a moment. As a young girl, she dreamed of living in America. When she left her homeland, skeptics thought she'd never make it. Her vision was to own land and be a successful business owner in the United States someday. The land was meant to leave an inheritance for her unborn children's children and the business was meant to serve the hearts and affect the lives of men and women in a positive way. Leaving her country with nothing but an attitude of determination and great expectations, she sought to bring her dream to fruition.

With nothing to call her own, she roomed with other newcomers, worked a lot, slept little, and learned a trade. Housekeeping, elderly and child care, and developing her professional skills quickly became her new way of life. Though challenged by immigration laws over forty years ago, she became a United States citizen. From there, she continued to strive with the expectation that realizing her dream would be inevitable if she held close to her faith and was committed to staying the course.

When she first worked in a professional atmosphere she was fortified in her spirit that she was on her way to the destination she believed God had ordained for her. Working to blaze a trail for herself and other members of her family, Leana's major concern was that of making an honest living she could be proud of. When she married and became a mother, she saw the pieces of her vision coming to pass. After saving, working, and strategizing, she purchased her first piece of property. Stopping at nothing less than what she allowed herself to envision, she soon purchased a home and started her own business.

For more than ten years she was the owner of a successful establishment that made a difference in her customers' lives and extended opportunities to young people in her field. It was a place to get advice, see a friendly face, rejuvenate, and leave looking and feeling better than when you came in. Despite what others saw or failed to see in her, she knew what she could accomplish if she held true to the vision, maintained the appropriate attitude, and expected nothing less than success. Just like she envisioned, she had dared to do it, and others were inspired when she did.

If you've had a vision but gave up on it, it's time to make the necessary moves to try again. Children, marriage, jobs, or age should not be used as excuses to give up. As a coach, I constantly hear one justification after another of why people are unable to pursue their passion. Using reasons to justify why they are living a life they don't want, just like that, the doors shut. After they reveal they are not where they want to be, I ask if they are willing to make small steps toward moving in purpose. Eliminating one "I couldn't" and an "I could never" after another, they start to embrace the idea that ingenuity, faith, and a strategy go a long way. They realize that no one benefits from an unfulfilled life. And, it is much better to make steps toward fulfilled purpose than more steps toward further unhappiness.

The choice to listen to your heart, write your personal vision, develop an action plan, investigate your potential resources, and give your best effort to follow through while embracing the journey, is the most optimal one you can make.

Vision starts with God and manifests itself through us. We either breathe life into it or it dies. I believe death and personal choice are the only things that can keep you from purpose. It's up to you to take every opportunity necessary to explore and move within the journey of realizing and manifesting what we were put here to do. As we embark on the journey, the vision may change; however, you must continue to strive knowing that you'll gain invaluable insight through every step of movement toward your God-appointed destination.

THE KEY IS NOT TO ALLOW YOURSELF TO THINK ABOUT WHY THE VISION CAN'T BE REALIZED, WHY IT'S A STUPID THOUGHT, WHY IT'S NOT THE BEST TIME TO TRY, WHY YOU COULD NEVER SUPPORT YOURSELF DOING IT, OR WHY THE OBSTACLES ARE TOO BIG.

The key is not to allow yourself to think about why the vision can't be realized, why it's a stupid thought, why it's not the best time to try, why you could never support yourself doing it, or why the obstacles are too big. When I embraced my passion for music and empowering others, I wasn't clear about how the two would come together, but I was open to cultivating them separately. I decided to major in psychology and joined a musical theater guild to get me started. I began to seek opportunities that would allow me to manifest the goals of singing and speaking to affect the lives of others in a positive way.

As I embraced my vision (the what), I still needed to figure out the how, when, and where. Interestingly enough, the how was an ever-evolving answer. When I began my journey, I prayed that the necessary tools to solidify it would be revealed to me. I couldn't decide how I would reach out to people. Where would I find receptive audiences that would listen to a then eighteen-year-old? The answer was not cut and dry. I wasn't famous, highly educated, a life coach, or even old enough to be considered a true adult. Who would want to listen to me? Not knowing it, I stumbled on one of the greatest obstacles in the vision process—the struggle with feasibility which speaks in term of likelihood and why things probably will or won't happen. With vision, feasibility can be the determining factor between movement and stagnation. It's up to you to dream beyond self-doubt and know that God would not give you an assignment for you to fail at it. So, push toward the mark and focus on doing all things with God on your side. As a young adult, I almost talked myself out of starting the cultivation process, but when I stopped embracing doubt and focused my determination, I started to seek doors to walk through.

To move beyond feasibility, I decided to explore several organizations that focused on the needs of women in my community. This search yielded an opportunity to volunteer at the domestic violence shelter I spoke of. Shortly after starting, I became a support-group facilitator. These groups of women became my first listeners and helped prepare me for what I do now. From that humble beginning, the domino effect toward the realization of my vision started to unfold. The same kind of opportunities became available with my singing as a result of being open and expectant.

Over time, those experiences became the building blocks that clarified the specifics of my purpose and continue to manifest my vision today.

Now it's your turn. If you are actively moving toward your vision, be encouraged. Your ability to envision great possibilities for your life is exactly what God intended. And for those of you who still don't believe, what would be the absolute worst thing that could happen if you moved toward making your vision a reality? When you saw the cover of this book, you saw my name and decided I was an author. I became an author the day I discerned that writing books was a vision God had for me. I envisioned the book's completion even as I faced a blank computer screen. The fact that you are reading *A Woman's True Purpose* is a testament to what God can do with a willing vessel. So, how much longer will you wait? It's time to stop standing on the sidelines of your own life. Write the vision, make it plain, and watch where God will take you as a result of your obedience.

SEVEN CRITICAL REMINDERS FOR YOUR JOURNEY FORWARD

- Vision is the projection of your destination (what is to come). It's up to you to embrace, see, and declare it.

- Attitude and expectation dictate the probability of your vision coming to fruition. The attitude that your dream can be manifested and the expectation that it will be manifested are critical.

- You cannot envision something great when you accept that there is no greatness in you. There is no such thing as a small purpose. A limited attitude and limited expectations will equal a limited vision.

- Believe in your God-view, embrace that God values you, and know that you are deserving of a God-given vision for your life.

- Where you are doesn't matter as much as where you see yourself going. Attitude and expectation are tied to the understanding that you are chosen; thus, the right woman for your God-given purpose.

- If you've had a dream but gave up on it, give it another try. Don't think about why it can't happen or why the obstacles are too big. Your ability to envision great possibilities for your life is exactly what God intended.

• As you embark on the journey, the vision may change; however, you must continue to strive knowing you'll gain invaluable insight moving toward your God-appointed destination. Take every opportunity necessary to explore and move within the journey of realizing and manifesting what you were put here to do.

INSIGHT CORNER

1. When you listen to what your heart has to say, what vision comes to mind?

_____

_____

_____

_____

2. What is your vision statement? (For example, I want to _____ through the use of my _____ for the good of _____.)

_____

_____

_____

_____

3. List five short-term goals to help you move from where you are to manifesting your vision statement.

_____

_____

_____

_____

4. What actions will be needed to fulfill your short-term goals (e.g., what, when, where, and how)?

_____

_____

_____

_____

a. What resources will you need to help you achieve your goals (e.g., who and what)?

_____

_____

_____

_____

b. What is your timeline for accomplishing these goals (e.g., start date/completion date)?

_____

_____

_____

_____

c. How will you know when your short-term goals have been met/achieved?

_____

_____

_____

_____

_____

5. List five intermediate goals to help you move from where you are to manifesting your vision statement.

_____

_____

_____

_____

6. What actions will be needed to fulfill your intermediate goals (e.g., what, when, where, and how)?

_____

_____

_____

_____

a. What resources will you need to help you achieve them (e.g., who and what)?

_____

_____

_____

_____

b. What is your timeline for accomplishing these goals (e.g., start date/completion date)?

_____

_____

_____

_____

c. How will you know when your intermediate goals have been met/achieved?

_____

_____

_____

_____

7. List five long-term goals to help you move from where you are

to manifesting your vision statement.

_____

_____

_____

_____

8. What actions will be needed to fulfill your long-term goals?

_____

_____

_____

_____

a. What resources will you need to help you achieve your goals (e.g., who and what)?

_____

_____

_____

_____

b. What is your timeline for accomplishing these goals (e.g., start date/completion date)?

_____

_____

_____

_____

c. How will you know when your intermediate goals have been met/achieved?

_____

_____

_____

_____

9. Identify one person who can be used to support your vision and share it with them. Be sure that this person has a good sense of wholeness because you don't want your efforts to be sabotaged as a result of another person's insecurities. Ask them to partner with you and help keep you accountable to your goals, plans, and personal timeline.

_____

_____

_____

Get in the Moment, It's All You've Got

Chapter 11:

FEAR AND ADVERSITY ARE NEVER REASONS ENOUGH TO QUIT

HAPPINESS VERSUS SADNESS, GOOD versus evil, open versus closed—all of these represent the law of opposites suggesting everything has two sides. These phrases categorize how we view many occurrences in our everyday lives. Positive sides of the law are deemed blessings, good fortune, and success, while the negative sides are perceived to be obstacles and misfortunes. The negative sides, or what I call the adversarial bumps of life, present the most challenge. None of us are strangers to adversity. In fact, many of us probably know adversity on a first-name basis.

Whether met in the form of injustice, lack of resources, or unfortunate circumstances, we know the results of adversity better than we care to admit. In our battles with life's ups and downs, some are classified as victories and others surrender, but all show varying levels of casualty and survival. Unfortunately, our fortitude and natural ability to overcome obstacles are often overshadowed and forgotten—not by others but by us. In battles to achieve wholeness, our own power is often overlooked. When required to exert the same stamina with which we fight for others—for ourselves, we often doubt our own abilities. That's because many of us build our combat strength in situations and events that do not consciously promote personal evolvement. As a result, when we have to fight to better ourselves, it can seem like frightening and unfamiliar territory.

For example, if a friend came to us feeling that she wasn't strong enough to complete her education, chances are we would encourage her, challenge her, and convince her that she had what it takes to reach her goal. Reminding her of past accomplishments, we would probably build a solid argument for why she was strong enough to pursue her dreams. However, when it comes to ourselves, our self-dialogue can be a lot less convincing.

For many women, this stance is most prevalent on the battlefield en route to fulfilling purpose. The purpose battle is different than most because it's all about you. Having fought this battle myself, I can only liken it to fighting for a championship title. Every champion conditions herself for battle. Steps One through Five in this book encourage the preparation for this battle on many different fronts. And, victory is solidified by our belief that we are worthy of achieving the life for which we were created. However, this belief does not negate the fact that part of the human experience includes experiencing bouts of adversity along the way. For the most part, we can expect adversity to promote chaos, doubt, and destruction. But most of all, we can expect it to show up in a form that is known by a single four-letter word: fear.

I once heard someone say fear is false evidence appearing to be real. It sounded clever, then it fostered a larger thought. If fear is false evidence and not real, why do we choose to give it so much power? Think about it; without your permission, fear can do nothing. To produce power and momentum, it needs your energy. Yet we empower it and continue to navigate our lives in accordance with it.

As a result, our list of fears go on and on. Whether you consider fear to be a force of nature, a spirit, or just a feeling, fear is one of our biggest adversaries. At different points in our purpose-led journey, fear will come and knock on our door seeking our attention, and here are what I consider to be the three favorite ways fear seeks to attack us.

WHETHER YOU CONSIDER FEAR TO BE A FORCE OF NATURE, A SPIRIT, OR JUST A FEELING, FEAR IS ONE OF OUR BIGGEST ADVERSARIES.

First and foremost on the list is fear of the unknown. Almost every coaching client struggles to resist turning this fear into a ten-foot giant. So here's an exercise: Take out a piece of paper, and in perfect detail, write down what will happen throughout the world between 8:00 and 8:05 tomorrow morning. Surely you can give an accurate account of what will happen—it's only five minutes. Attempting to do so, you will discover exactly what I did.

Every single moment, minute, and second of the day make up a part of the unknown. At best, you may have a calculated guess, but you are no more in control of predicting the unknown with one hundred percent certainty than I am of predicting whether or not you will choose to live like you matter. So why let this fear be an inevitable part of your existence? Instead, why not recognize your power to influence the unknown instead of fearing it?

For example, when taking a test, at best you may have an idea of what type of content will be assessed. However, agonizing over not knowing the exact questions will not change the fact that they'll be unknown until they're sitting in front of you. So spending your energy studying and praying for strength to influence the outcome is a much more powerful strategy for conquering this unknown.

When we look at vision as it relates to the unknown, sometimes the only part of the vision we can see in the moment is the "what" (e.g., destination), but the "how" (e.g., detailed aspects of the necessary journey) remains unknown. In those cases, we have to trust that God sees everything, so our best bet is to move with the end in mind—all the while accepting that the rest of the journey, like the next five minutes of your life, will remain unknown until experienced. In these situations, it is imperative we do not allow fear of the unknown to stop forward movement. Besides, how will your vision ever be fully realized if you let this fear have its way?

As seen in this next case, fear of the unknown almost had an undeserved victory. Holly enjoyed working in the competitive world of finance for years before acknowledging her passion for working with kids. Being a successful career woman in corporate America, she couldn't imagine what it would take to move off her already solidified path and make a drastic career move. Though holding a coveted position and having achieved the respect of her peers, she became more in tune with the fact that she wasn't living within her purpose. When she explored the idea of changing careers, fear of the unknown was her biggest adversary. How would her personal finances be affected by the change? How would she make the transition? How would life as she knew it be different?

Would it be worth it? Would she regret it? Would she be good at it? What if changing her career turned out to be a mistake? For Holly, fear of the unknown manifested itself in a barrage of questions that sought to debilitate her effort to move forward.

As a result, her first step was recognizing she had no guarantees when she moved into the financial industry nor did she have much of a passion for it; however, she still managed to thrive. She survived, having dealt with a great many unknowns. So, what might be possible if she had a great deal of passion, a purpose driven vision, and the same level of unknown? What could be possible if she committed to giving the same energy, but this time, headed toward something she genuinely loved and was authentically inspired by?

With that, her declared vision to become a teacher was no longer one she chose to denounce. Instead of fearing the unknown, she sought to research the process and manage the unknown as much as possible. For almost a year, she investigated her options and made strategic moves to leave the financial industry. Now, despite the ups, downs, and sacrifices of being a teacher, I've heard her say, "I love teaching" and "You couldn't pay me to go back to Corporate America" on more than one occasion. In overcoming her fear of the unknown, she was able to realize her dream.

The second fear on my list is the *fear of failure*. Many of us fear failure to the point of being willing to settle for one of the truest forms of failure—not trying at all. Like fear of the unknown, we give the fear of failure the power to paralyze us rather than daring to do something that might potentially place us in the path of success. With a mastery of excuses and justifications, we convince ourselves that doing nothing is better than giving our all and not getting the outcome we desire. Here's the kicker: What most consider to be failure is almost guaranteed under those circumstances. You won't have to fear failure; you'll experience it firsthand. Why not fully engage, dare to step out on faith, and cover as much ground as possible? True, you may not always end up where you want to be, but is that failure? I beg to differ.

MANY OF US FEAR FAILURE TO THE POINT OF BEING WILLING TO SETTLE FOR ONE OF THE TRUEST FORMS OF FAILURE— NOT TRYING AT ALL.

Maybe it's time we reevaluate what failure is so we can have a better understanding of why fear of it is so counterproductive. For example, if you were in a hallway of fifty doors and one door held your fulfilled vision, failure would not be defined by finding that door on the fiftieth try. Failure would be the decision to not open all fifty doors because you considered trying every door to be too emotionally taxing. What's the worst that could happen? Like life, all forty-nine doors before the jackpot were part of the critical journey toward your jackpot—door number fifty. So, a willingness to take the journey is key to the victory. Door number thirty was no more a representation of failure than door number forty-nine. On your journey to a successfully manifested vision, what you'll find is that every step along the path offered insightful lessons about yourself, what to do, what not to do, and what tools needed to be used to get you to your God-ordained destination. As in the following example, we all must take steps to travel beyond where we are.

Theresa decided to become a stay-at-home mom after the birth of her son. A dedicated wife and mother, she committed herself to being at home with her two boys. When her kids were in middle school, she was nudged by the option of going back to work or to school to further her education. When we explored her heart's desire, she became immediately overwhelmed. She admitted to a long-standing dream of becoming an engineer. For Theresa, fear of failure had become a great deterrent. Now in the prime of her life, it was still working overtime. Her fear had now fostered a belief that her family would be negatively affected by such a commitment, she would never be accepted to engineering school, and even if she did slip through the cracks, she would be setting herself up for embarrassment. In fact, she was so fearful, initial conversations about the possibilities prompted her to disconnect from our relationship.

After months of no contact, she initiated contact with a nervous willingness to break through and engage in the ride of discovery wherever it would take her. In doing so, she embraced her commitment to try. Investigating engineering programs in her area she took a courageous step and enrolled in the necessary pre-requisite classes to start preparing for potential enrollment. Boldly moving toward her dream, her renewed confidence and process toward acquiring this degree has continued to soar.

The third fear on my list is the fear of success. I, too, have been guilty of being debilitated by the thought that the light of my spirit could positively affect the lives of others in a big way. That should be a good thing, yet the fear of success all too often, overwhelms many of us. This was definitely the challenge in Camilla's situation.

When I saw her, it was hard to ignore that Camilla was anointed with a gift of dance that touched the heart. However, when we met, she was overwhelmed by a fear of success. She recognized her gift, but was terrified of where it might take her and whether or not she could live up to God's standard for her talent. As a result, she attempted to downsize her blessing by not accepting the fullness of it. Her vision—to use her life to share the concept, word, and glory of God through dance—was clear, but she never felt worthy or capable of bringing it to fruition. In a sense, she was somewhat blinded by her own light and the calling on her life.

When placed in the midst of plentiful opportunities to spread her wings and move into her rightful position, she often felt out of sorts and found it hard to recognize that she belonged. She belonged because God had already defined her belonging. When we spoke about inviting her fear on her journey until she felt strong enough to eliminate it, Camilla was confused as to what that would look like. Once she committed to try, she started welcoming versus dreading opportunities to cultivate her talent. With a desire to overcome her fear and gain momentum, she willingly accepted opportunities to display her gift. As a result of her movement, her fear of success became less of a deciding factor in whether or not she moved forward.

What I found through this encounter was invaluable, a major problem with the fear of success is two words—accountability and responsibility. Would success mean you could no longer accept less than your best, give less than your best, be less than you best? Probably! But here's the conundrum: How is accepting less than your best, giving less than your best, and being less than your best been pleasing to God or beneficial to others?

For Camilla, she had to accept that accountability and responsibility existed in both doing nothing and doing what she was called to do. Therefore, she would rather be accountable and responsible for something that could inspire and change the lives of others than continue being irresponsible and accountable for her own paralysis. When she dared to move out of her own way she started to live the life to which she was born—one in ministry on a stage she was meant to command.

Like most fears, fear of the unknown, fear of failure, and fear of success never travel alone. They creep around with their buddies: fear of inadequacy and fear of greatness. Together, as a team, they seek to convince us that shrinking and hiding would be better than striving to give our internal brilliance an opportunity to shine on the world. But isn't that why God gave us purpose, to use our lives as an extension toward the greatness of humanity? Who, exactly, does denouncing or avoiding our internal light help?

It is not arrogant to believe you can improve the world by fulfilling your purpose and being engaged in loving and living to the fullest. Instead it's one of the most humanitarian things we could hope to do. When we serve in the capacity God intended, it is service well placed. In a nutshell, decisions like that of fearing success may fit with our self-view, but it has no place with our God-view.

Fear is not an unconquerable beast.
It's more like a deceptive coward
that seeks to worm its way through
us, influence our decisions, and take
over our sense of faith and logic.

Yes, fear in its many forms may drop by unannounced and uninvited, but as previously mentioned, we are not obliged to let it in. And, if we do, we have the power to make the visit brief and kick it out at any time we choose. Fear is not an unconquerable beast. It's more like a deceptive coward that seeks to worm its way through us, influence our decisions, and take over our sense of faith and logic. It tries to limit where we'll go and tell us what we can't do.

Not surprisingly, fear never tells us what we can do. It never gives us anything positive in return for the room and board extended. It never cheers our efforts. It continuously undermines who we really are so we'll never reach our true potential. Fear is not there to tell us, "God sees you as a treasured investment," "You'll never know unless you try," "You've been through worse and came out swinging," and "God sees greatness in you." Instead, it attacks with words like unworthy, impossible, and unfeasible. Well, if these words were enough to stop us, we would never see acts of greatness, not to mention miracles. As I see it, winners have three things to say to fear:

- I won't be afraid of you.
- Get behind me; you have no control over me.
- You may have slipped in, but you can't stay here.

The first two are rather self-explanatory. As for the third, however, here is what I mean: at times fear will creep in through a back door and try to seek permanent residence. It does so because it figures once it's in, it can stop progress. When this happens, what should we do? We should move forward anyway and take fear with us until we can kick it to the curb.

FEAR DOESN'T LIKE MOVEMENT. BECAUSE I WENT FORTH ANYWAY, FEAR LOST ITS STAYING POWER.

I experienced this firsthand when I took my oral examination to receive my PhD. The mere thought of standing in front of a room full of professors turned me into an emotional basket case. Yet, I had only two choices: take the exam or retreat. Though I decided to take the exam, I will admit I let fear come along for the ride. Through that experience, however, I learned an important lesson: fear doesn't like movement. Because I went forth anyway, fear lost its staying power.

As I stood before scholars whose experiences and knowledge base were vastly beyond my own, I let my faith take flight. As I advanced through one question after another, my fear had no choice but to flee. On that day fear came with me, but it couldn't stay. What fear had attempted to convince me I couldn't do, faith and God-given courage helped me accomplish, with honors and distinction.

Yet again, I found the use of faith, persistence, and hard work to be trusted weapons that can endure in any battle. Not only are they necessary, but they solidify a conviction that we can be victorious and engender a spirit of boldness to walk forward. As we seek to live purpose-led lives, we must dismiss the notion that purpose never includes struggle. Purpose is in no way exempt from life's bumps and bruises. I can't stress it enough, if we have to experience adversity as an overall part of living, it seems more strategic to experience it while journeying toward purpose versus a life we're settling for.

Living in our purpose will take work and commitment, but what doesn't? If adversity is not enough to make you quit when it comes to other parts of your life, it should not stop you when it comes to living within your own purpose. Life's trials and tribulations are not a permission slip to give up. If you don't believe me, think of it this way: At any given point in your life, you are either entering a storm, in the midst of a storm, or moving out of a storm. With each move, your objective should be to press forward as the wind and rain try to push you backward. If you don't allow yourself to be consumed with fear, you can march forward knowing the pressure will eventually decrease and cease. So the question is, are you ready to stop looking at the obstacles as defining moments and look at them as mere bumps along the way?

In life, there is no such thing as an indefinite setback or failure because every lesson learned up to that point can be used to maximize future efforts. It's up to us to look beyond the walls that appear to be made of stone and kick them down. Your heart can be trusted. Whatever God placed in it is a desire that the universe is waiting to be fulfilled.

I once heard someone say eagles are special because they, unlike other birds, can soar toward the sun, without being affected by its glare. As symbols of strength, their best viewpoint is from above and they dare to embrace brilliance. That's why our God-view is so important. That view never bows to adversity; it stretches forward and beyond it. So what will you choose to do?

SEVEN CRITICAL REMINDERS FOR YOUR JOURNEY FORWARD

- Your fortitude and natural ability to overcome obstacles should never be forgotten. Victory is first determined by your own belief that you are worthy of achieving it.

- Facing misfortune on the journey toward prosperity is inevitable, and you can expect to have challenges along the way. Knowing this, it's important to be aware of adversity in the form of fear.

- Be sure to not let fear of the unknown, failure, or success get the best of you. Together, they seek to convince you that shrinking and hiding would be better than striving to give your internal brilliance an opportunity to shine on the world.

- To combat adversity, use the weapons of faith, persistence, and hard work to endure the battle and win.

- If adversity is not enough to make you quit when it comes to other parts of your life, it should not be enough to stop you when it comes to living within your own purpose.

- Life's trials and tribulations are not permission for you to give up.

- In life, there is no such thing as an indefinite setback or failure because every lesson learned up to that point can be used to maximize your future efforts. It's up to you to look beyond the walls that appear to be made of stone and kick them down.

Insight Corner

1. As it relates to your journey toward personal purpose, what obstacles and bouts with adversity have deterred your efforts?

_____

_____

_____

_____

2. How can you use previous victories and triumphs as tools of motivation in your journey toward purpose?

_____

_____

_____

_____

3. What kind of support system can you create to encourage yourself when you feel like giving up?

_____

_____

_____

_____

4. What action(s) will you take to put this support system in place? Who will you ask to be your accountability partner in this journey?

_____

_____

_____

_____

Chapter 12:

RUSHING THROUGH YOUR LIFE PROFITS NO ONE

"WHERE WERE YOU? I WAS BUSY. Busy doing what? I was busy getting to the next there. Besides, who has time to be here when you still have the next there to get to?"

IT'S A KIND OF TUNNEL VISION THAT PLACES A SPOTLIGHT ON THE DESTINATION AND RENDERS THE JOURNEY A NECESSARY INCONVENIENCE.

That wasn't a dialogue between two people—it was a conversation between me, myself, and I. It was a critical and unforgettable conversation that caused me to pause and reflect on how I was moving through my own life. I diagnosed it as my own personal "just passing through versus being fully present syndrome." It's a kind of tunnel vision that places a spotlight on the destination and renders the journey a necessary inconvenience.

More and more we're buying into lifestyles that endorse running a race without paying attention to anything other than the finish line. This cycle of racing to complete one goal after another perpetuates a lack of presence that makes some of life's most valuable moments nothing more than a blur. Ultimately, it serves to cheat many of us of moments I believe God wishes we would cherish and pay attention to.

I learned this lesson the hard way. As you look at the cover of this book, you'll see the book title, but you'll also see my name with two little letters in front of it: "Dr." It still pains me to admit that I missed most of the doctoral journey. But I did. Like many other things in my life, I wanted it, pursued it, and achieved it.

During this process, I focused on the challenges in front of me and fought to stay one step ahead of the game. I was always sure to juggle more than one goal at a time. Regardless of my accomplishments, I just kept on going. Rarely did I come up for air and take into account the obstacles I successfully overcame. Once the race began, completing the goal quickly and efficiently became the coveted destination. Having yet to enter superwoman recovery, I rarely took into account the gifts within the journey. In doing so, the essence of the experience almost passed me by and made for an anticlimactic ending.

Like other challenges, once the race began, completing the goal quickly became my point of focus. However, the challenges within the journey and my determination often worked together to render me emotionally absent from many of the successes along the way. As a result, achievements that should have been eventful, like receiving my master's degree, were just a matter of process.

IT IS UP TO ME TO TAKE ACCOUNT OF THE
HERE AND NOW WITH PASSION AND
DELIBERATE INTENT AND USE IT TO
CELEBRATE MY THERE AND TOMORROW.

For me, finishing my master's degree just promoted the question, "How much further to the doctorate?" I was so on the move, I didn't even consider going to the master's graduation ceremony. The sad thing is, I can't even tell you what I did on the day of the ceremony. I got so caught up in the final destination, I missed some of the best parts of the journey. I missed the part where you say to yourself "great job," the part where you take a moment to look at how strikingly fabulous you really are as a woman, the moment where you recognize your blessings and reward your efforts. In my eagerness to arrive at the destination, my appreciation for the process and myself was often rushed or, worse yet, overlooked.

The experience of acquiring my doctorate taught me many things. For starters, the physical aspects of any journey are an inevitable requirement (studying, gaining practical experience, taking exams); however, the recognition of personal triumphs and successes along the way should never be passed by. Even in times of turmoil, they offer gifts of joy to behold, but the decision to embrace, devalue, or ignore them on the way to the next challenge is a personal one.

I also learned that time will keep ticking whether or not I take a moment to embrace the fullness of my own life and all the experiences, joy, and laughter within it. It is up to me to take account of the here and now with passion and deliberate intent and use it to celebrate my there and tomorrow. As we move from one accomplishment to another we must recognize our presence is necessary. Living like we matter requires that we stop to smell the flowers. And, all parts of the journey (the beginning, middle, and end) require your presence, not just the ultimate destination.

NOW SHE EXPERIENCED BOTH GOD AND BEING ALIVE AS THE ENCOURAGEMENT NEEDED TO TAKE NOTHING AND NO ONE FOR GRANTED.

When Helen was stricken with breast cancer it never occurred to her how priceless the little things were. After her mastectomy and successful chemotherapy, we spoke about how life had changed beyond the obvious. More than anything she spoke of having a keen sense of self and everything around her. She felt her blessings more intensely and recognized that her views on many things had taken a significant turn. Now she experienced both God and being alive as the encouragement needed to take nothing and no one for granted. She could see things so clearly and I likened her explanation to what I imagine a person might see if they were given sight after blindness—witnessing a cluster of images and stimuli that only they could appreciate having once been unable to see them.

In a strange way, the cancer that was meant to destroy her saved her life by opening her eyes. Before her illness she was indeed a fighter, but too often she missed the little things that she didn't need to fight for—the things that just wanted to be noticed. In remission, being present in her relationship with God and all that her senses can bare has become the difference. She now stands in alliance with other women as they band together to fight the war on cancer and view every day of presence as a priceless gift—the gift of being alive.

As a woman, your presence validates that you are indeed embracing life in its entirety. It reminds you to be the first to acknowledge your blessings. It encourages you to validate your own achievements, see the victory in your own battles, and most of all, it designates that you are indeed the best note taker of your own life.

YOUR ASSIGNMENT IS NOT TO BE PERFECT. YOUR ASSIGNMENT IS TO BE PRESENT, PASSIONATE, AND PURPOSEFUL.

Who takes good notes for us when we are absent from our own lives? What does it profit us to surpass much of life's dialogue and only have an accomplishment to show for it? How can we help others go down our once traveled path if we have little recollection of it? Our presence is not just important for our own level of insight and fulfillment, it's critical to the journey of other human beings who will seek to go where we've been. When you stop to smell the flowers in your life, it helps to call attention to the same fragrance in the lives of others.

Your assignment is not to be perfect. Your assignment is to be present, passionate, and purposeful. With an inability to see into the future, it's impossible to know which experiences are most valuable and most important. Therefore, we must choose to acknowledge every moment we can. For all of us, life lessons are determined by the journey. When we own all we have to be grateful for and extend thanks for the multiple blessings within every day, triumph, and journey, the destination becomes more like the icing on the cake. To miss it would mean missing the insight and "Aha" that often make for the sweetest memories and, quite frankly, some of the most heartfelt laughter.

ACKNOWLEDGING "HERE" IS THE BIGGEST PART OF WHAT MAKES "THERE" SO INCREDIBLE.

If you are presently reading this chapter and saying to yourself, "I'll make time the next go around," "I'll get to it when I get through this crunch period," "On my vacation I'll take some time," STOP! Stop and ask yourself why you are choosing not to fully engage in your own life. This is not about vacations or getting through one last deadline. It's not okay to be asleep behind the wheel of your life.

No matter the goal, obligation, responsibility, or expectation—ownership and recognition of your happiness is the foundation from which all other potential sources of fulfillment will flow. So, dare to be present within your here and now. It's no longer okay to walk through a garden and not smell a flower. Don't miss the opportunities for laughter when you hear something funny. Don't skirt past an emotion to avoid feeling exactly what you feel. Don't miss the joy you feel when you care enough to help someone.

On a very basic level, it's all about truly embracing the subtleties in all of life's splendor. So as you strive for your goals, nurture your families, and make a difference in this world, dare to look around and receive all that deserves to be noticed. As you do, you may find acknowledging "here" is the biggest part of what makes "there" so incredible.

Seven Critical Reminders for Your Journey Forward

- It's not okay to be asleep behind the wheel of your own life. No matter the goal, obligation, responsibility, or expectation—ownership and recognition of your happiness is the foundation from which all other potential sources of fulfillment will flow. So, dare to be present.

- Being present is a divine assignment in which you're called to cherish all that God wants you to, so don't miss it by racing to the next goal.

- You are the best note taker of your own life. Your presence is not just important for your own level of insight and fulfillment; it's critical to the journey of others who will seek to go where you've been.

- When you own all that you have to be grateful for and extend thanks for the multiple blessings within your journey, the destination will become more like the icing on the cake.

- When you stop to smell the flowers in your life, you'll help call attention to those same fragrances in the lives of others.

- Don't miss the parts of the journey where you applaud and say to yourself "great job"; the part where you take a moment to look at how strikingly fabulous you really are as a woman; the moment where you recognize your blessings and reward your efforts.

- Don't be so eager to arrive at the destination that you negate the process and forget to appreciate who and where you are.

Insight Corner

1. List at least three positive moments within the past two years that didn't receive the fullness of your presence, time, and recognition. What did you learn from not doing so?

_____

_____

_____

_____

2. What are some things in your life that deserve to be noticed on a daily basis but don't get the attention they deserve? What can you do to practice embracing the moments of the present instead of instantly racing toward the next challenge?

_____

_____

_____

_____

3. What can you do to be in a state of gratitude for all that surrounds you in your present journey?

_____

_____

_____

_____

4. What can you do to start being more attentive and committed
to smelling the flowers every day, thus promoting a continuous
sense of presence?

_____

_____

_____

_____

RENEW YOUR SWEET SPOT

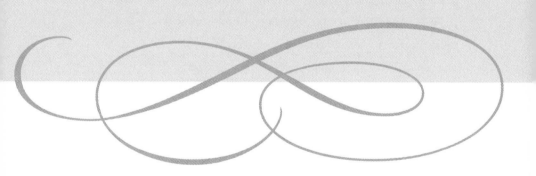

Chapter 13:
Today Is...

LIFE IS INDEED FUNNY. Maybe it's because the journey from here to there is a never-ending cycle that presents every day as another chance to follow our heart, move beyond basic survival, and embrace personal peace. Every day is yet another opportunity to ask the tough questions and embrace truthful answers. Having moved seven steps forward, you've gone too far to turn back now. Knowledge is power and the subject matter is you. Who better to choose than you? Choose to live! Not tomorrow or next week, today!

WE, TOO, MUST BREAK THROUGH TO THE ENDLESS POSSIBILITIES THAT SEEK TO MOVE US FROM BASIC SATISFACTION TO A HIGHER SENSE OF PURPOSE, CONNECTION, AND AUTHENTICITY.

Minute by minute, the world as we know it changes, like we do. As each day presents new challenges and a hopeful step closer to our goals, we are given the charge to embrace the ride and take good pictures of the view. If we're true to the process of personal discovery and jump in with both feet, there promises never to be a dull moment.

We can look forward to numerous quests and even expect an epiphany or two along the way. If we're lucky, the insight received will bring us closer to an appreciation of just how special we really are. The voyage is there to promote growth, not a jaded reality. Like a seed that's planted and breaks through the earth to blossom into its fullness, we, too, must break through to the endless possibilities that seek to move us from basic satisfaction to a higher sense of purpose, connection, and authenticity. Every day is a new day of commitment to being our best. Despite what did or didn't happen yesterday, today is a new beginning.

For me, February 15 will forever be my special today. Unexpectedly, this day brought forth a gift of hope I shall never forget. As I moved from one meeting to the next, I pondered what I would say. When I called Mrs. McIntosh to announce I would be late, I couldn't help but think of their faces. How did I want our time to be remembered? Would my presence make a difference? The whole way there I experienced anxiety about my tardiness being a reflection of not caring or recognizing their importance. As I rushed up the stairs, I tried to stay calm; I walked through the double doors then down the hall, took a deep breath, and prepared to enter into the moment.

When I opened the door, there they were, a roomful of them. Seeing their eyes filled with curiosity, their excitement matching mine, I felt honored. There I was, entering a bulletin board-filled classroom to experience the enthusiasm of fifth-grade girls awaiting my arrival. They were my dream audience. So impressionable, so open, so optimistic…but what I prepared to say seemed unbefitting. As I scrambled to rethink my presentation, we talked about their educational foundation and I praised their potential. With sincere curiosity I inquired about what they wanted to be when they grew up and listened to dreams that made me proud. Their innocence and enthusiasm took me back twenty years. They had a pure and unadulterated sense of optimism and belief in the possible; they were in their sweet spot. A space where they were passionate about life, free to believe God had called them to greatness, and willing to love and laugh with an endless innocence.

I RECEIVED AN OPPORTUNITY TO SEE HOPE AT ITS BEST, A ROOMFUL OF POTENTIAL, SHOUTING THIS PHRASE AT THE TOP OF THEIR LUNGS, AS IF IT WERE A POWERFUL MANTRA.

Collectively, they had big dreams and a sense of fulfillment and happiness yet untarnished. Their hearts were in full conversation and they saw no need to censure. As I listened to them, it occurred to me that they saw every day as a new day. No matter their home life or what was going on in the world, each morning offered another chance to dream, laugh, live, and love. This premise alone made their futures full of promise.

Well, I had dared to think it, so I took a chance and said it: "Today is the first day of the rest of your life." Then it happened: In that moment, I received an opportunity to see hope at its best, a roomful of potential, shouting this phrase at the top of their lungs, as if it were a powerful mantra. As they screamed, "Today is the first day of the rest of your life" over and over, it occurred to me that I was the one who needed to hear it. I watched them screaming it as if they were trying to convince me to capture the moment in my heart and share it with every woman as a special message from them. It was as if they knew that I, like many of you, needed not only to hear it but to own it.

As I listened, I wished that every day would reinforce this empowering belief for myself and for them. Through the future pains, disappointments, and obstacles I wished that they would continue to view each day as a renewed first day to see the value of their dreams—that every "today" would be embraced as one full of possibilities for forgiveness, overcoming adversity, and living within purpose. That every "today" would give them an opportunity to leave yesterday behind, embrace their God-view, and experience God's love.

I COULD EMBRACE THE WOMAN
I WAS BORN TO BE, DREAM BIG, LIVE
PASSIONATELY, LOVE UNCONDITIONALLY,
LAUGH OFTEN, AND MAINTAIN A SENSE OF
WHOLENESS WITH NO REGRET OR SHAME.

What I wished for them I needed to reaffirm within myself. On that day I went to inspire and instead received inspiration. On that day, the phrase that is often overused seemed different. In its simplicity, it seemed like, for the first time I truly understood what it meant—I could dare to renew my fifth-grade spirit. I could embrace the woman I was born to be, dream big, live passionately, love unconditionally, laugh often, and maintain a sense of wholeness with no regret or shame.

In one visit, a group of girls reaffirmed everything I had spent months writing about. In that one day they reinforced my belief that attitude is truly the first step toward the most positive outcomes. It was indeed true; my thoughts did have the power to influence, control, and manifest my every day. The brilliance within them was unwavering. In a very real sense, I could see in them the ability to be anything and go anywhere.

Their belief in themselves would give them authority over their personal journey, and their spiritual connection would help determine their bumps along the way. What their tomorrows would bring, no one would know, but how they received their challenges would establish their ability to take life by storm. With profound clarity I saw them as examples to live for and live by. In them, I saw how powerful the phrase "today is the first day of the rest of your life" really was. Simply, it offers a lifetime of grace, mercy, and choices, despite moments of the past. It begs that you take a chance and choose yourself because you are truly the best thing that could have ever happened to you. You are on the planet Earth because you still have greatness to explore, treasures to give, and more life to live.

In one moment, a group of fifth-graders validated what my spirit had struggled with most of my adult life: that purpose, wholeness, and fulfillment are daily choices every woman has to make to live her life to the fullest. Every day presents another opportunity to not give up on being your best self. Each dawn is filled with the opportunity for a new outlook. As they jumped up and down and stretched their arms as if they could reach the sky, they suggested it was time to seek what we wanted out of life and stand within our God-given light.

THEY SUGGESTED IT WAS TIME TO SEEK
WHAT WE WANTED OUT OF LIFE AND
STAND WITHIN OUR GOD-GIVEN LIGHT.

As I remember their faces, I recognize that their innocence had a flame of bravery and entitlement toward good that could only be dimmed by future experiences seeking to wound their self-esteem. For them, unworthiness would be their threatening illusion. However, each of us would have an opportunity to protect and secure them through our own living example. Our actions could make the difference for them.

What if we stopped wishing that yesterday could be different? If we stopped living for other people's expectations and respected our own? If we stopped working hard for things we didn't want and redirected that energy to do things that mattered to our hearts? If we stopped being so hard on ourselves and taking ourselves for granted? If we stopped perpetuating the mundane and belittling our strengths? What if we started to show them how to live by letting go of the past and embracing every day as a blessing? If we started to make choices that celebrated our womanhood? What if we started to give ourselves the best and let our faith overwhelm our fears? What if we embraced our purpose daily, loved the women we were unconditionally, laughed a little more, and cried a little less?

If we stopped certain things and started others, I dare to think they would have an even greater chance. A chance to know that aspiring to be like us is not a misguided aspiration. Don't they deserve that? It's all up to us now. What will you choose to do? Will you choose to live? Will you choose to live like you matter? I sure hope so. After all, no one has ever been more worth it!

Today is…

Insight Corner

1. Viewing today as the first day of the rest of your life, what written commitment will you make to:

a. Believe the power of your God-view

_____

_____

b. Take charge of your past

_____

_____

c. Embrace the potential of resolution and forgiveness

_____

_____

d. Stop being invisible

_____

_____

e. Move in the divine direction

_____

_____

f. Get in the moment

_____

_____

g. Renew your sweet spot

_____

_____

2. Viewing today as the first day of the rest of your life, what will you do to embrace the woman you were born to be and to live like you matter?

_____

_____

_____

_____

3. What will you do to make the most of every day from this moment forward?

_____

_____

_____

_____

Acknowledgments

One morning while driving, the vision of this book started to take shape. From that day forward, I embraced the journey of transforming my thoughts into written words. Thank you all for supporting me in this endeavor.

My husband, Calvin: God gave me a true confidant and friend in your arrival. You continue to stand thirteen feet tall in my eyes. I truly love you!

My mother, Pearl: Words cannot express my gratitude for all the love and support you've given me. Thank you! Thank you! Thank you!

My father, Leroy: Thanks for showing me the power of forgiveness and resolution. May we continue to grow and move forward in a Godly direction.

Faithful Central Bible Church (FCBC): Bishop Kenneth C. Ulmer and Lady Togetta, thanks for being an example to the masses. Bishop, your leadership and powerful sermons have strengthened my spiritual walk more than you will ever know. Pastor Charles Brooks, you are a wonderful man of God. Let your light shine so that all may know He Lives. Dr. Kenneth Polite, it is an honor to learn from you; thanks for guiding, teaching, and pulling me in.

The FCBC staff: The body of Christ is blessed to have your dedication; it is an honor to serve with you.

The FCBC encouragers: Strong, wise, kind, and committed; thanks for covering me in prayer.

Pastor Joann, Yolanda, Brittany, Gail, Chrystal, and Gina: Thanks for praying and pulling out the words to draw women closer to their personal truths.

Pastor Benny Hinn, Bishop Eddie Long, and Reverend Norman Owens: You were the start of my spiritual maturity and I thank you for introducing His light and helping me to be accountable to His word.

Sara Camilli: You're the best agent I could have hoped for. Thanks for representing and believing in me. Here's to the future!

Thanks to Deb Werksman, Rebecca, Leigh, and the entire Sourcebooks staff.

All the aunts (you know who you are): Thanks for your continuous love and care—you just keep on blessing me.

Auntie Meema: Thanks for always being there and all you've done. Chow Chow. I'll try to keep you laughing. Auntie Greta and Pat: Thanks for being such godparents. Auntie Angie: Thanks for being different than the rest. Tantie Pheta: I honor you. Auntie Gloria, Phyllis, and Marcel: Thanks for the love.

My cousins: No matter the distance, you are but a phone call away (thanks for being there). Michelle, we have to move closer, luv ya.

My Sisters, Brothers, and God Children: What a blessing you have been to me. I thank God for blessing me through each and every one of you.

My executive and life coaching clients: Serving you has been one of my greatest joys. You are all powerful and blessed individuals to behold. Cheers and a million thanks.

My Friends: May our friendships continue to grow and manifest for God's pleasure. Joelle and John: I can't wait for Greek2Be to take off. Thanks for the love and undying support. Grafton: Your help and friendship is priceless. Tomorrie: I couldn't have done the book or the wedding without you. Heather, Big Sis: Thanks for having such a big heart. Kelly: Thanks for the trip to Cali, luv ya. Kim, Scott, and Cynthia (Cyndi): I love and thank you for still being my friends. Lucious, Chrystal, Vonda, Camille, Ogden, and Janice: Your prayers, love, support, and friendship are truly appreciated.

Dr. Richard Harvey: Thank you for being my earthly angel—love the "Little D."

Travis Hunter: Thanks for taking the time to help a new author learn the ropes. You were a treasure during this process.

Elicia Wood: One billion thanks could never be enough. I'll never forget!

Andrea Tyndale, Chandra Sparks-Taylor, John P., Christopher Pike, Launi Wilson and Jason Medley, Trina Broussard, Crysta Bragg, Michael Motta, and Emilia Serrano: You helped bring the pieces together—my sincere gratitude.

Carlos Arriaga and Alice Furlow: I am still missing you.

The focus group readers in St. Louis and Los Angeles: Thanks for using your wisdom and discernment to help me complete this work.

Spelman College: The place where young women blossom into great women. Thanks for grooming me. Cheers to you!

Starbucks: Who knew I would write this entire book in such a great place. Your employees are truly the best.

The Inn On Summer Hill: Thanks for being a good place to gather my thoughts.

To all the other people who helped along the way: Your belief in me made touching the lives of many a possibility.

About the Author

Dr. Nicole LaBeach is a sought after consultant and the CEO of Volition Enterprises, Inc., a premier personal and professional coaching and development firm. As former Director of Training and Organization Development for Fortune 500 company News Corporation (parent company of all Fox entities), her coaching and consulting career includes work with professionals and executives from 20th Century Fox, Fox Sports, Fox Searchlight, Anheuser-Busch Corporation, and Southwestern Bell, respectively. Executive and life coach to diverse corporate, entrepreneurial, faith-based, and entertainment clients, Dr. LaBeach has promoted positive and significant change in the personal and professional lives of both men and women.

Dr. LaBeach received her doctorate in Organizational Psychology and master's in Research, with a concentration in Clinical Psychology, from Saint Louis University in St. Louis, Missouri. Her undergraduate education in psychology was completed at Spelman College in Atlanta, Georgia. Her diverse clinical background as a therapist culminated in her position as the Associate Director of Counseling at Faithful Central Bible Church in Los Angeles, California. In this capacity, her work with individuals, couples, and families within the ten thousand member congregation and greater Los Angeles community was a genuine passion. Dedicated to the empowerment of the human spirit, Dr. LaBeach is a dynamic and charismatic speaker who stands on the premise "Life is a Gift. Living is a Choice."

A native New Yorker, born to Caribbean parents, she maintains a bicoastal residence in Florida and California with her husband, Calvin. You can visit her website at www.volitionenterprises.com